BATTLESHIPS
OF WORLD WAR I

BATTLESHIPS
OF WORLD WAR I

OVER 185 ARCHIVE PHOTOGRAPHS AND ILLUSTRATIONS OF 70 SHIPS

Peter Hore

southwater

This edition is published by Southwater
an imprint of Anness Publishing Ltd
Hermes House
88–89 Blackfriars Road
London SE1 8HA
tel. 020 7401 2077; fax 020 7633 9499

www.southwaterbooks.com; www.annesspublishing.com

Anness Publishing has a new picture agency outlet for images for publishing, promotions or advertising.
Please visit our website www.practicalpictures.com for more information.

UK agent: The Manning Partnership Ltd, 6 The Old Dairy,
Melcombe Road, Bath BA2 3LR; tel. 01225 478444;
fax 01225 478440; sales@manning-partnership.co.uk

UK distributor: Grantham Book Services Ltd, Isaac Newton Way,
Alma Park Industrial Estate, Grantham, Lincs NG31 9SD;
tel. 01476 541080; fax 01476 541061; orders@gbs.tbs-ltd.co.uk

North American agent/distributor: National Book Network,
4501 Forbes Boulevard, Suite 200, Lanham, MD 20706;
tel. 301 459 3366; fax 301 429 5746; www.nbnbooks.com

Australian agent/distributor: Pan Macmillan Australia,
Level 18, St Martins Tower,
31 Market St,
Sydney, NSW 2000;
tel. 1300 135 113; fax 1300 135 103;
customer.service@macmillan.com.au

New Zealand agent/distributor: David Bateman Ltd,
30 Tarndale Grove, Off Bush Road,
Albany, Auckland;
tel. (09) 415 7664; fax (09) 415 8892

Publisher: Joanna Lorenz
Senior Managing Editor: Conor Kilgallon
Senior Editor: Felicity Forster
Copy Editor and Indexer: Tim Ellerby
Cover Design: Jonathan Davison
Designer: Ian Sandom
Production Controller: Pedro Nelson

ETHICAL TRADING POLICY
At Anness Publishing we believe that business should be conducted in an ethical and ecologically sustainable way, with
respect for the environment and a proper regard to the replacement of the natural resources we employ. As a publisher,
we use a lot of wood pulp to make high-quality paper for printing, and that wood commonly comes from spruce trees.
We are therefore currently growing more than 500,000 trees in two Scottish forest plantations near Aberdeen –
Berrymoss (130 hectares/320 acres) and West Touxhill (125 hectares/305 acres). The forests we manage contain twice
the number of trees employed each year in paper-making for our books. Because of this ongoing ecological investment
programme, you, as our customer, can have the pleasure and reassurance of knowing that a tree is being cultivated on
your behalf to naturally replace the materials used to make the book you are holding. Our forestry programme is run in
accordance with the UK Woodland Assurance Scheme (UKWAS) and will be certified by the internationally recognized
Forest Stewardship Council (FSC). The FSC is a non-government organization dedicated to promoting responsible
management of the world's forests. Certification ensures forests are managed in an environmentally sustainable and
socially responsible basis. For further information about this scheme, go to www.annesspublishing.com/trees

© Anness Publishing Ltd 2006

Previously published as part of a larger volume, *Battleships*

1 3 5 7 9 10 8 6 4 2

PAGE 1: *Ise.* PAGES 2–3: *Von der Tann.* PAGE 5: *Oklahoma.*

Contents

Introduction

A basic style of sailing ship, capable of taking part in battles – or a "line-of-battle ship", from which the term "battleship" is derived – dominated warfare at sea from the 16th to the 19th century. Then, just as the British Navy celebrated her sea victory in 1805 at the Battle of Trafalgar, new technology became available which revolutionized battleship design. This revolution encompassed the use of steam engines at sea, breech-loading guns, rotating turrets, armour and, above all, an increase in ships' size. The developments were so frequent and numerous that at one stage a British prime minister complained that ship design was a changing fashion, like ladies' hats.

The battleship itself, broadly defined here as a capital ship mounting guns of 255mm/10in calibre or more, took on many different shapes for the first 20 years of its life. Designers faced difficult choices, weight being a primary driver in the decisions which had to be made. For example, many early designs had large, heavy barbettes, which meant a low freeboard and loss of sea-keeping; the alternative was a high-sided ship with a resulting loss of stability. This period was marked by some exceedingly odd and ugly ships.

There were developmental dead ends as well. The paddle ship, with its exposed wheels, was useless as a vehicle of war – the paddlewheels and boxes were too vulnerable to damage and restricted the size of broadside armament that could be mounted. However, the paddle ship was useful for towing sailing ships into action.

TOP: *Erin* was originally built for the Turkish Navy and paid for by public subscription. Britain requisitioned her, and the resulting outrage helped bring Turkey into the war on the side of the Central Powers. ABOVE: This view of a *Delaware*-class Dreadnought clearly shows the lattice or cage masts that were favoured by US Navy designers during the early Dreadnought period.

Other lines of development took unexpected turns. The monitor was designed for coastal defence and for war in estuaries and rivers, and was highly successful in the American Civil War. However, when given a little more sea-keeping capability, monitors became powerful weapons of offence, mounting some of the largest guns taken from their "big sister" battleships. In two World Wars, monitors were used in operations from the Arctic to Africa, and indeed at the end of their lives the shore-bombardment role of some battleships could be compared to that of an over-large monitor.

By the end of the 19th century the design of the battleship had more or less settled on a ship of about 10,160 tonnes/ 10,000 tons, carrying two twin barbettes or turrets, one forward and one aft, and sometimes with side-by-side funnels. Their speed of 18 knots was considered fast.

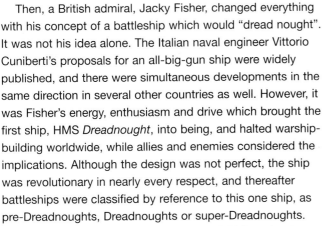

Then, a British admiral, Jacky Fisher, changed everything with his concept of a battleship which would "dread nought". It was not his idea alone. The Italian naval engineer Vittorio Cuniberti's proposals for an all-big-gun ship were widely published, and there were simultaneous developments in the same direction in several other countries as well. However, it was Fisher's energy, enthusiasm and drive which brought the first ship, HMS *Dreadnought*, into being, and halted warship-building worldwide, while allies and enemies considered the implications. Although the design was not perfect, the ship was revolutionary in nearly every respect, and thereafter battleships were classified by reference to this one ship, as pre-Dreadnoughts, Dreadnoughts or super-Dreadnoughts.

Once the 20,320-tonne/20,000-ton and 20-knot barrier had been broken, development continued apace, and within 10 years, subsequent generations of Dreadnoughts had reached 30,480 tonnes/30,000 tons and 30 knots. Other developments included the re-introduction of secondary armament to deal with the increasing threat from torpedo boats, and in some cases the main armament was mounted in triple turrets. Furthermore, as the value of aircraft at sea was increasingly recognized, battleships were fitted with flying-off ramps. Finally, new engine technology allowed oil to begin to replace coal as the preferred fuel.

The Battle of Jutland in 1916 was the only large-scale fleet action involving battleships of the Dreadnought type, although minor actions involving battleships of this era took place across

ABOVE LEFT: *Iron Duke* served as Admiral Jellicoe's flagship at the Battle of Jutland. TOP: Battleships which maximized the number of guns that could be brought to bear on a target were deployed in the line of battle. ABOVE: *König* was also present at Jutland, where she was heavily engaged.

the globe throughout World War I. Battleships were also tasked with providing naval support for amphibious troop landings and raids, as well as more general shore bombardment missions.

This book looks first at the fascinating history of the battleship, from the development of the first Dreadnoughts through to the end of World War I, and identifies those individuals who were responsible for bringing about the revolution in battleship design. It also chronicles the main battles and naval operations of World War I, concluding with the scuttling of the German High Seas Fleet at Scapa Flow. The country-by-country chronological directory that follows describes the most famous ships of this type that took part in the conflict from the main naval powers, notably Britain, the United States, Germany, France, Italy and Japan, as well as those of the smaller navies. This, then, is the story, told through the lives of individual ships, of the development and deployment of one type of ship which dominated naval strategy from 1906 through to the end of World War I.

The History of World War I Battleships

The term "battleship" derives from "line-of-battle ship", meaning a ship strong enough to fight in the line of battle, the ultimate expression which started with the revolutionary new design seen in HMS *Dreadnought*. Developed in 1906 as a single ship rather than a class, this unique vessel gave its name to a new type of battleship that dominated the future development of capital ships worldwide and rendered all other previously built battleships redundant.

This book tells the story of the technological developments that led to the creation of *Dreadnought,* together with an account of the people who had the vision and drive to make it happen. Critical naval engagements and operations of World War I are also highlighted, including accounts of the only large-scale fleet encounter at Jutland as well as the fate of the German High Seas Fleet at Scapa Flow.

This was a golden age for the battleship and Dreadnought type in particular, but the source of its demise soon made its presence felt as the torpedo and ship-borne aircraft became significantly more reliable and effective.

LEFT: **HMS *Vanguard,* a member of the third class of basic British Dreadnoughts to be built, approaching Portsmouth.**

Cuniberti, Scott and Sims

In addition to Fisher, three men stand out as having strongly influenced the development of the big gun and the design of the *Dreadnought*. The Italian naval architect and engineer Vittorio Cuniberti was descended from a successive line of innovative Italian naval architects such as Brin and Micheli. At the beginning of the 20th century Cuniberti had drawn up plans for a ship with a single calibre of big guns, but the project was regarded as too ambitious for the Italian navy, and in 1902 he was given permission to publish an article in *Jane's Fighting Ships*, then a newly established publication. The article was entitled: "An Ideal Battleship for the British Fleet" and his ideas were for "a moderate-sized, very swift vessel with the greatest possible unified armament". An article that was published three years earlier in German in the *Marine Rundschau*, "Ein neuer Schlachtschifftypus" had attracted little attention, but by 1904 navies around the world were about to analyse the Battle of Tsushima and its implications for warship design.

At this time guns were laid by eye, so the direction officer needed to see the fall of shot in order to estimate the range adjustment. Cuniberti and others appreciated that as guns of all calibre improved and could be fired to the limits of visual observation it was increasingly difficult to distinguish the fall of

ABOVE: **Cuniberti's ideas were taken up in several countries, where some smaller navies did not slavishly copy Fisher's Dreadnought but designed all-big-gun ships from first principles, like the small but purposeful and elegant *España,* seen here.**

one shot and thus make the appropriate corrections. Cuniberti actually lampooned the American practice of fitting up to four different calibres, writing, "Looking to America, one realizes that chaos reigns in the designing department of the United States Navy, and hardly a month seems to pass without a new type being brought out, more and more loaded with guns." Whether Cuniberti's ideas actually influenced any British decision or the ideas arose spontaneously and simultaneously in different navies is not known but Fisher was the first to implement them.

Meanwhile in the Royal Navy, Percy Scott was improving the accuracy of gun laying. Scott is best known for his efforts during the Boer War in 1899 when as captain of the cruiser *Terrible* he designed makeshift gun carriages for the ship's guns so they could be taken up-country by a naval brigade to help the army at the siege of Ladysmith. He was training commander at the gunnery school, HMS *Excellent*, in

Portsmouth, 1890–3, a member of the Ordnance Committee, 1893–6, captain of HMS *Excellent* in 1904, and Inspector of Target Practice in 1908, and in 1916 he was called from retirement to create the Anti-Aircraft Corps for the defence of London against air attack. Scott was a prolific inventor who devised a loading tray to teach faster loading, a "dotter" designed to help his gun layers record accurate bearings, and introduced director firing from a centralized position in the ship. The gunnery technology of the day was capable of firing a shell ten miles, and Scott helped the Royal Navy to hit targets at these ranges more accurately. After the war he argued that the advent of submarines and aeroplanes meant that the day of the battleship, which his inventions had helped to perfect, was over.

William Sims, a Canadian by birth, joined the USN and between regular appointments was a naval attaché in Europe. Sims reported on new ship designs and improvements in gunnery and wrote directly to President Theodore Roosevelt criticizing the efficiency of the USN. He supported Roosevelt in arguing for the USN adopting an all-big-gun Dreadnought fleet against others, including the now elderly Mahan who advocated a mixed calibre and a "balanced fleet". Roosevelt made Sims his protégé and he went on to introduce the continuous aim method developed by Scott to the USN. He commanded the battleships *Minnesota*, 1909–11 and *Nevada*, 1916–17. Sims was briefly president of the US Naval War College but in March 1917 he was made the USN's representative in London. When the USA entered World War I he took command of all American destroyers operating from British bases, helping to establish convoys to overcome the strangulating effect of German U-boats. Like Scott he became an apostate regarding battleships and in retirement was an advocate of naval aviation. Despite the contributions these men made, the modern battleship is indelibly linked with Fisher and his *Dreadnought*.

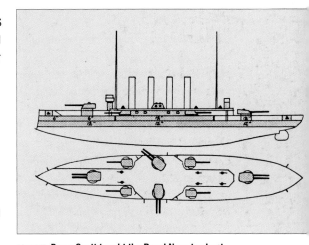

TOP LEFT: **Percy Scott taught the Royal Navy to shoot and he was a prolific inventor. He later argued against the retention of the battleship because it was rendered obsolescent by new weapons.**
TOP RIGHT: **As a junior officer William Sims supported Theodore Roosevelt by advocating an ocean-going fleet.** ABOVE: **A line drawing of Cuniberti's proposed all-big-gun battleship: even Cuniberti retained some smaller guns, essential for anti-torpedo defence. His proposals, however, did not go as far as having the guns on the centreline so that they could all be brought to bear on one target.**

Goeben and battleships in the Black Sea

The bombardments by the German Admiral Wilhelm Souchon of the French ports in North Africa at Bône and Philippeville on August 3, 1914, were the first shots of the war at sea in World War I. His subsequent escape through the Mediterranean was a disgrace to the all-powerful Royal Navy and the arrival of his modern battlecruiser at Constantinople later that month brought Turkey into the war on the side of the Central Powers. Souchon's bombardment of Odessa on October 29 opened the war between Turkey and Russia, but, when he met a squadron of Russian pre-Dreadnoughts in the Black Sea, Souchon failed to use his speed and firepower to destroy his foe.

At the outbreak of war Souchon commanded the only German ships in the Mediterranean, the modern battlecruiser *Goeben* and the light cruiser *Breslau*. His orders were to cooperate with the Austro-Hungarian and Italian fleets and interdict the passage of French troops across the Mediterranean. When Austria declared war against Serbia on July 28, *Goeben* and *Breslau* were at Pola and by August 1, when Germany declared war on Russia, Souchon's ships had moved to Brindisi, where, fearing internment after Italy had declared its neutrality, he sailed west in the direction where the Royal Navy thought he might make for the Atlantic. Though Britain had yet to join the war, the battlecruisers *Indomitable*

ABOVE: The German *Goeben*, having altered the balance of power in the Dardanelles and Black Sea, hoisted the Turkish flag and was briefly captured at Novorossiysk before being handed back to the Turks in November 1918.

and *Indefatigable* looked for Souchon, and met him on August 4 returning eastwards. Both sides were at action stations but their guns were trained fore and aft, and as the British turned to follow, Souchon increased speed and gradually lost sight of the British battlecruisers.

Souchon coaled at Messina, feinted towards the Adriatic and headed for the Dardanelles: he was found again by the Royal Navy which acted timidly and he escaped to Constantinople. Meanwhile on August 2, two Turkish battleships completing in British yards, *Resadiye* and *Sultan Osman I* (formerly the Brazilian *Rio de Janeiro*), were confiscated by the Royal Navy and commissioned as *Erin* and *Agincourt*.

On August 16 Germany announced the sale of Souchon's squadron to Turkey as *Sultan Yavuz Selim* and *Middilli*, Souchon became commander-in-chief of the Turkish battlefleet and his German crew continued to man their ships.

On November 18, 1914, *Goeben* intercepted the Russian battlefleet consisting of the pre-Dreadnoughts *Estavii, Ioann Zlatoust* (both 1903), the 1905 *Pantelimon*, the 1895 *Rostislav*,

and the 1891 turret ship *Tri Sviatitelia* returning from bombarding Turkish positions. Souchon was eager for a fight and expected to find the Russians easy prey, but he was unpleasantly surprised by the weight and accuracy of the Russian fire.

Poor visibility eliminated *Goeben*'s guns' range advantage, and the Russians, who had learned some lessons from their defeat at Tsushima, were practised as a centralized firing unit. This meant that the centre ship in a three-ship group would pass ranges and bearings to coordinate the fire of the other ships. The older *Rostislav* and *Tri Sviatitelia* were not part of the firing unit and were free to fire on *Breslau*.

In the quarter hour's engagement which ensued, at ranges of 5–8km/3–5 miles, *Breslau* took shelter on *Goeben*'s disengaged side from the hail of fire and *Goeben* was hit 14 times, mainly by *Evstafii*. *Evstafii* was hit four times before *Goeben* veered off into the mist and did not attempt to renew the engagement.

Thereafter there was stalemate in the Black Sea, and *Goeben* did not challenge the Russian pre-Dreadnought Black Sea Fleet. While the Russians operated as a squadron they were relatively free to bombard Turkish ports and positions until even *Goeben* was affected by coal shortages.

After many other actions, *Goeben* and *Breslau* sortied from the Dardanelles to raid Salonika on January 20, 1918, where they sank the British 355mm/14in gun monitor *Raglan* and the smaller 235mm/9.2in gun *M28*. *Breslau* was mined and sunk and *Goeben* was beached after hitting three mines herself. She was repaired in time for the surrender of the mutinous Black Sea Fleet on May 2, 1918.

Rebuilt in 1927–30, and again in 1938 and 1941, she was renamed *Yavuz Selim*. The ex-*Goeben* was offered back to

TOP: **A close-up of *Goeben* after turrets while under military guard. Presumably no officer is watching this man smoke.** ABOVE: ***Goeben*, the ever-elusive German battleship, at last in British hands. From her escape from the Royal Navy in the Mediterranean in 1914 until the Armistice in 1918, *Goeben*, whether she was German or Turkish, had a major impact on the strategic balance in the Black Sea and altered great power politics.**

Germany in 1963 but the offer was refused and so after a period as a museum ship she was scrapped in 1976. Souchon's own career ended in ignominy when in late October 1918 he was removed from his command at Kiel by mutineers.

Jacky Fisher

Jacky Fisher, or Admiral of the Fleet Lord Fisher of Kilverstone, was the father of the Dreadnought revolution, a revolution which changed naval warfare and the balance of power between nations. Fisher linked the old sailing navy with the new, having been nominated by the last of Nelson's captains. As a young officer he served in the Crimea and in China at the battle of Fatshan Creek. Specializing in gunnery, he served on *Warrior* when she was new, and was responsible for a number of innovations including the introduction of electrical firing circuits in the guns of *Ocean* in 1869, and helped to found the Royal Navy's experimental school in HMS *Vernon*. Later he commanded the battleship *Inflexible* at the bombardment of Alexandria in 1882 and took command of the Naval Brigades when they landed.

As Director of Naval Ordnance Fisher introduced a range of modern weapons to the Royal Navy and as an admiral he was responsible, as Third Sea Lord, for delivering the ships ordered under the Naval Defence Act of 1889. Whilst serving as Commander-in-Chief, Mediterranean, he concentrated on firing at long ranges, taught the fleet to manoeuvre in tight formations at maximum speed, and studied the tactics that this implied. Then as Second Sea Lord he reformed the officer and rating structure and training which he implemented whilst Commander-in-Chief, Portsmouth.

From the 1880s onwards Fisher increasingly turned to politics to promote the Royal Navy and his ideas, using his friendship with the journalist W T Stead. He also made influential friends in royal circles and amongst politicians, particularly Winston Churchill.

Fisher brought this powerful suite of technical, strategic and political skills, together with his forceful character, to the office of First Sea Lord in 1904. He advocated the use of submarines and ensured that at the outbreak of World War I the Royal Navy had one of the largest fleets of submarines. Whilst in the Mediterranean he had conceived the idea of the large armoured cruiser, which became the battlecruiser, and though he could not solve the problem of ships having to fight in line-of-battle, he proposed the creation of mixed "fleet units". In response to the danger posed by the rise of the German fleet, Fisher concentrated the Royal Navy in home waters, and needing the manpower for new, larger warships, he controversially paid off many older ships on overseas stations as they were too weak and too slow. Above all, however, Fisher pressed for speed and hitting power in warships.

LEFT: **A famous picture of Fisher's protégé, John Jellicoe, mounting a ladder onboard the battleship *Iron Duke*. Jellicoe was a man consumed by self-doubt, despite the impression of dynamism given by this picture.** BELOW: **An unusual picture of Fisher relaxing with visitors onboard the battleship *Renown*.**

The concept of the all-big-gun battleship was not new. The Italian designer Vittorio Cuniberti had written about it and been published in Germany and Britain, and similar ideas were being developed in the USA. Fisher's critics said that by building the all-big-gun battleship he made every other battleship obsolete including all the Royal Navy's, but it seems that it was an idea whose hour had come, and for once the Royal Navy was first. *Dreadnought* was Fisher's brainchild and it was his fanatic drive and energy which made the development time so short: within months he had decided upon the 305mm/12in gun armament and opted for every innovation available, Professor Barr's 2.74m/9ft optical rangefinder accurate to 6,400m/7,000yd, steam turbines rather than reciprocating engines, and enhanced underwater protection. By robbing the Lord Nelson class of their guns Fisher was able to claim that he had built *Dreadnought* in twelve months and she was officially completed on Trafalgar Day 1906. However, Fisher also made personal enemies, and was forced to retire in 1910, continuing to give advice from retirement in France. He became mentor to Winston Churchill when he was First Lord of the Admiralty, and it was under his tutelage that Churchill persuaded the British government to take a stake in the Anglo-Iranian Oil Company (which grew into British Petroleum) in order to ensure oil supplies for the Royal Navy. Then, after Prince Battenberg was forced to resign as First Sea Lord in 1914 on grounds of his German background Fisher was recalled. As First Sea Lord he was responsible for sending battlecruisers to the South Atlantic in response to the German victory at Coronel, but subsequently fell out with Churchill over his interference in operational matters during the Dardanelles campaign, and resigned.

Fisher was also responsible for advancing the career of John Jellicoe. Jellicoe was not an inspirational leader like Fisher and failed to make best use of his ships when Fisher's mighty fleet of Dreadnoughts was tested at the Battle of Jutland in 1916.

ABOVE: **Jacky Fisher, as he was universally known, seized upon good ideas and turned them into his own but he also had the energy and force of character to make them happen.** BELOW: **Fisher had many ideas, including the concept of a fleet unit and the battlecruiser, and he was an advocate of the submarine. But his greatest brainchild, for which he is best known, was *Dreadnought*, a new type of warship that made all preceding battleships obsolescent, and from which the type took its name.**

The Anglo-German naval race

In the early 20th century the Royal Navy was at the height of its power, was superior by a ratio of two to one to any other navy, and had been at peace for the best part of 100 years – there had been no general war since 1815. The French navy had not really been a threat for many years, and the Russian navy had suffered a crushing defeat at Tsushima in 1905 by the Japanese navy which was under British tutelage. However, the German navy was beginning to grow and establish overseas bases, and the United States Navy (USN) had shown its potential by the cruise of the Great White Fleet in 1907–9.

Royal Navy relations with the USN were cordial and Sims, for example, had been one of the first foreign visitors to inspect *Dreadnought*. On a personal level many British and German officers knew and liked each other, but relations with the German state deteriorated. Kaiser Wilhelm II and naval chief Admiral von Tirpitz wanted a modern navy for personal and prestigious reasons as much as for securing an overseas empire, and they wanted a large navy even if this meant challenging the Royal Navy. The Kaiser's brother, Prince Henry of Prussia, who was also an honorary Admiral in the Royal

ABOVE: **As well as Dreadnought-type battleships, the German navy also employed airships to carry out reconnaissance for the High Seas Fleet.** BELOW LEFT: **Grand Admiral Alfred von Tirpitz who encouraged the German Kaiser to challenge the Royal Navy by building up a "Riskflotte", which helped bring about World War I.**

Navy, made the German navy a respectable profession for ambitious young Germans, while the Kaiser ordered the works of the American naval strategist, Captain Mahan, to be translated and placed in the wardrooms of all his ships. Wilhelm II had absorbed the lesson from his reading of Mahan that a large navy and great power status were synonymous. Perhaps also his cousins on the British throne with their command of the Royal Navy gave him an inferiority complex. The Kaiser was ably assisted by Tirpitz, who had joined the Prussian navy in 1865 and then the navy of the new German Empire when it formed in 1871. Tirpitz, who had commanded the East Asiatic Squadron in 1896–7 when a treaty was concluded with China, returned to Berlin to commence his challenge to the Royal Navy by building up the German navy.

Up until the 1890s the German navy had been a coastal defence force. However, harnessing German industrial power, new German Navy Laws in 1898, 1900, 1908 and 1912 envisaged a balanced fleet which by 1920 would include 38 battleships. Tirpitz's concept was of a *riskflotte* or risk fleet: he reasoned that Britain would not go to war with Germany if Germany possessed a significant fleet, because, although the Royal Navy would win any campaign at sea, it would be so weakened that the two-power standard would be broken and Britain exposed to defeat at sea by France, Russia or even the USA.

RIGHT: **This photograph dated November 28, 1918, shows the German fleet at Scapa Flow after the British Grand Fleet had escorted it into internment.** BELOW: **King Edward VII of Great Britain and his nephew Kaiser Wilhelm II of Germany – it was partly Wilhelm's jealousy of his uncle which drove him to build up the German navy. Books have been written about the extent to which Anglo-German rivalry was a personal affair between the British and German royal families, and a political inevitability of German reunifications in the late 19th century.** BELOW RIGHT: **The German navy at Kiel before World War I, making its challenge to the Royal Navy.** BOTTOM: **This photograph is entitled "the last [large calibre] firing of the German fleet" and shows the effect of firing a broadside – and the resulting smoke. The extent of the German challenge to Britannia's rule of the waves was taken seriously by the Royal Navy.**

The result was somewhat different. Britain became concerned that German naval expansion would provoke French and Russian shipbuilding, and therefore concluded a treaty with Japan. The treaty allowed the Royal Navy to maintain only token forces in the East, and other steps were taken to reduce British imperial commitments: Jacky Fisher brought many ships home from their overseas stations, and paid off older warships to man the new. The larger countries of the British Empire were urged to help create an empire navy by establishing their own navies, like the Royal Australian Navy. Then in 1904 Britain unexpectedly joined in an *entente cordiale* with her long-time enemy, France, and, after the annihilation of the Russian navy at the Battle of Tsushima, Britain and Germany were left to face each other across the North Sea. The launch of *Dreadnought* in 1905 temporarily halted battleship building in Germany, while the German navy designed new ships, but once the naval arms race started afresh it became one of the catalysts of World War I. As war loomed, the French navy was persuaded to concentrate its forces in the Mediterranean, while the Royal Navy took on the defence of the North Sea and northern France.

Despite the efforts of Wilhelm II and Tirpitz, the German battleship building programme never came near to matching the Royal Navy and the challenge tailed off with the approach of war as the German army diverted resources from Wilhelm's navy. In the same period 1907–16, USA completed 14 battleships, Japan and France seven each, Italy and Austro-Hungary five each, Brazil and the Argentine two.

The Battle of the Falklands

The Battle of the Falklands in 1914 was regarded as a triumphant vindication of Jacky Fisher's much-criticized concept of the battlecruiser, a name given by the British Admiralty in 1911 to a new class of heavily armed cruisers.

The outbreak of World War I found Admiral von Spee, commanding the German East Asiatic Squadron, cut off in the western Pacific, with half the world and the Royal Navy between him and home. Without supplies of coal Spee's chances of reaching Germany were slim, and he headed for the west coast of South America, detaching one cruiser to make a diversion into the Indian Ocean. The British divided their forces, and a mixed squadron of elderly ships under Admiral Cradock entered the eastern Pacific. The German squadron contained two large vessels, *Scharnhorst* and *Gneisenau*, which were crack gunnery ships. When Cradock clashed with Spee's squadron off Coronel, the Germans were able to hold him at long range, and the British cruisers *Good Hope* and *Monmouth* were sunk on November 1, 1914.

This blow to British prestige unleashed all the latent energy and resource of the oldest and most powerful of the navies. All available cruisers were ordered to concentrate in the River Plate, and from Britain, two of the latest and fastest battle

ABOVE: **The battlecruiser *Invincible* was flagship of the British squadron at the Battle of the Falklands in December 1914. Admiral Sturdee's rapid deployment to the South Atlantic, ordered pre-emptorily when more work was still needed in the dockyards at Devonport, was timely and he beat the German admiral to the Falklands by only a few hours.**

cruisers, *Inflexible* and *Invincible*, were detached from the Grand Fleet and hurried south under the command of Admiral Sturdee – both battlecruisers still had some dockyard mateys working onboard. Sturdee's order gave him an almost free hand, and, as Commander-in-Chief South Atlantic and Pacific, the largest geographical command ever entrusted to a single admiral. The British force concentrated at the Abrolhos Islands and then steamed on southwards with the ships formed in a scouting line at 19km/12-mile intervals.

Sturdee's ships arrived at the Falklands on December 7, 1914, and as the British coaled their ships, the Germans arrived the following morning. As Spee turned away, his ships belching black smoke, Sturdee ordered his ships to sea and the chase began with the Germans already hull down on the Southern horizon. Spee ordered his light ships to make for South American ports whilst the *Scharnhorst* and *Gneisenau*

prepared to take on the British battlecruisers, who, each flying three ensigns, caught up and commenced firing shortly after 13.00. The Germans were in line abreast chased by the British in quarter line. The fall of shot threw up mountains of water, the peaks rising to over 90m/300ft above the water, but there were few hits at long range.

As Scharnhorst and Gneisenau turned to port, their firing was "beautiful to watch", with perfect ripple salvos all along their sides. A brown coloured puff with a centre of flames masked each gun as it fired, straddling the British ships, and causing splinter damage. In Inflexible, one officer noted, "We could hear the shells coming with a curious shrill whine which gradually got deeper and then pop, pop as they burst in the water". In the German ships the long-range plunging fire of 305mm/12in shells was devastating: one German survivor reported that he could feel his whole ship shake and the decks rippled like a caterpillar. At about 14.00 Spee altered course and drew out of range, but by 15.00 the British had closed the range again, and a fierce exchange began. At 15.40 Spee turned 180 degrees away, and Sturdee turned his ships together to port. Then at 16.20 the Scharnhorst suddenly turned over and sank.

TOP: **When Spee's German squadron was spotted approaching the Falklands, the British cruiser Kent was at anchor and so the first ship to get under way.** ABOVE LEFT: **Invincible making an immense amount of smoke in order to work to her full speed of 22 knots, and flying a battle ensign (probably taken from the cruiser Carnarvon).** ABOVE; **The German battleships Scharnhorst (seen here when new in 1910) and Gneisenau formed the core of Admiral von Spee's squadron, whose route home was barred by the Royal Navy.**

An hour later, after both British battlecruisers had concentrated their fire on Gneisenau, she too stopped, gradually turned over and sank. Over 2,000 men were killed in the blazing wrecks or drowned in the freezing waters. Only the German cruiser Dresden escaped from the Battle of the Falklands and she was to be hunted down later. Within months of the outbreak of war the German navy's attempts at commerce raiding using surface ships had been brought to an end.

The British battlecruisers had proved they could protect trade and pursue a fleeing enemy, but whether they could also provide a heavy scouting force to the main fleet or close support to the battlefleet would be proved at the Battle of Jutland in 1916.

19

New bottles for old wine

Even before their heyday at the Battle of Jutland in 1916, the construction of battleships was beginning to falter. In World War I Britain and Italy both had the same operational requirement to manoeuvre on the flanks of their armies and to bombard the enemy with heavy guns. Full-sized battleships, whether obsolete or not, were unsuitable to operate in shallow waters and so specialized ships were built. Although none of these ships bore any resemblance to the low-freeboard monitors of the previous century, the name "monitor" was applied to the resulting single-turret ships.

On the rivers and coasts of the northern Adriatic, the Italian navy converted barges captured from the Austrians into gun platforms, creating a class of monitor that was largely un-armoured. The largest of these were the *Alfredo Cappellini* and *Faa di Bruno,* which used the guns from the battleships *Francesco Morosini* and *Cristoforo Colombo.* The *Monte Santo* and *Monte Sabotino* had guns from the Caracciolo class of battleships, which had been cancelled in 1916.

In Britain, 355mm/14in guns intended for Greece were purchased from their American maker and fitted to the new monitors, which, presumably under Churchill's influence, were

given the names *Admiral Farragut, General Grant, Robert E. Lee* and *Stonewall Jackson.* However, following protests from the USA their names were changed to *Abercrombie, Havelock, Raglan* and *Roberts.*

During 1914 and 1915 the Majestic class of 1890s vintage pre-Dreadnoughts were laid up to provide their 305mm/12in guns for the Lord Clive class of monitors, this time all named after British generals. Three of these, *Lord Clive, Prince Eugene* and *General Wolfe,* were later fitted with a single 455mm/18in gun in a fixed mounting.

ABOVE RIGHT: **In the line of evolution of the battleship,** *Glatton* **(1871) represents an obscure type designed both for coastal defence and bombardment of the enemy coastal targets.** BELOW: **The Royal Navy took the concept of the coast attack ship and built a large number of monitors during World War I. One of the last of these was** *Terror,* **sunk in the Mediterranean in 1941.**

Strangely, the next two monitors were named after French generals, *Marshal Ney* and *Marshal Soult*. They were built with 305mm/12in turret guns taken from the battleship *Ramillies*, thus delaying her completion until 1917. Many smaller monitors were also built, including two coastal defence battleships bought from the Norwegians while under construction, *Gorgon* (ex *Nidaros*) and *Glatton* (ex *Bjorgvin*). Last, largest and most successful to be built were two 380mm/15in gun monitors, *Erebus* and *Terror*. *Erebus* survived torpedoing in 1917, but was sunk by a German dive-bomber off North Africa in 1941.

Characteristic of the new British monitors was their seaworthiness and they saw action in the Dardanelles, in the Adriatic and on the Belgian coast. At the end of the war some were sent to the White Sea and the Baltic to fight the Bolsheviks. Many of the new monitors also carried a single aeroplane for spotting the fall of shot, until they were replaced by shore-based aircraft of the newly formed Royal Naval Air Service. In World War I the Royal Navy led the world in naval aviation and two ships, the battlecruiser *Furious* and the battleship *Eagle* (formerly the Chilean *Almirante Cochrane*) were converted to aircraft carriers. *Furious*, designed as a light battlecruiser with two single 455mm/18in guns, underwent two conversions. In the first conversion she was given a flying-off deck by covering over her forecastle. The aircraft were then recovered from the water by crane after flying off.

In September 1917 she was taken in hand again, her remaining big gun removed and she was given a full length flightdeck. In June 1918 *Furious*'s Camel fighters drove off enemy aircraft and in July they successfully attacked Zeppelin sheds at Tondern in what must rate as the first carrier-borne aircraft strike. *Furious* also served in World War II.

In 1918 the partly completed *Almirante Cochrane* was also purchased for conversion to a through-deck aircraft carrier, although she was not completed until the 1920s. Amongst several other cancelled aircraft carrier projects, the first modern purpose-built aircraft carrier in the world was *Hermes,* laid down in 1918 and completed in 1924.

TOP: **While Germany concentrated on lighter-than-air machines, such as the Zeppelin, the Royal Navy developed the use of fixed-wing aircraft. At first each battleship and cruiser was fitted with one or two aircraft, but soon it was realized that a dedicated ship was needed. As the battleship approached its zenith, the Royal Navy began to build dedicated aircraft carriers. The light battlecruiser *Furious*, with her two single 455mm/18in guns, was converted in two stages.** ABOVE MIDDLE: **The after turret was removed to make a hybrid ship but this was unsuccessful.** ABOVE: **In 1917 she was fully converted before being completely rebuilt between the wars.**

In the USN a class of fast, heavy battlecruisers intended as a counter to the Japanese Kongo class and the British Hoods was cancelled. The two hulls were then taken in hand and built into aircraft carriers, the *Lexington* (CV2) and *Saratoga* (CV3). Likewise steel assembled for *Ranger* was used to build the USN's first purpose-built carrier. However the story of these ships belongs to another book. Aircraft carriers would replace battleships as the capital ships of the future.

North Sea actions 1914–15

The Battle of Heligoland Bight was the first major surface action at sea in World War I when, in late August 1914, Commodore Tyrwhitt, based at Harwich, conducted a sweep into the Heligoland Bight with cruisers and destroyers, while Beatty's First Battle Cruiser Squadron provided cover. On the morning of August 28 Tyrwhitt sank some torpedo boats but was soon outnumbered by the rapid reaction of German cruisers, and as Tyrwhitt fell back on the British battlecruisers, *New Zealand* and *Invincible* were damaged and the cruiser *Arethusa* had to be towed home. The German light cruisers *Mainz* and *Köln* were sunk and three other German cruisers were damaged, further enhancing Beatty and Tyrwhitt's reputations as fighting admirals.

Thereafter, the German tactics were to make raids into the North Sea with the hope of drawing individual British ships and formations into U-boat traps where the Royal Navy's numerical superiority could be whittled away until the German High Seas Fleet could meet the British Grand Fleet on more or less equal terms.

On December 16, 1914, the High Seas Fleet Scouting Group, as the German battlecruisers were known, bombarded the English east coast towns of Hartlepool, Whitby and Scarborough. Several hundred civilians were killed or wounded, though not without a coastal battery damaging some of the German ships including the armoured cruiser *Blücher*. Intelligence had given the Royal Navy warning of the raid and six battleships, four battlecruisers and several

TOP: **The German battle fleet during firing practice and manoeuvring for the photographer.** ABOVE: **The Dreadnought revolution coincided with the centenary of the Battle of Trafalgar in 1805, and the names of the new battleships reflect the Nelson age. This is the British battleship *Temeraire* painted by A. B. Cull.**

cruisers, under Admiral Warrender, were deployed. However, the German admiral, Hipper, and his battlecruisers *Seydlitz, Moltke, Von der Tann*, and *Derfflinger,* plus cruisers and destroyers, was covered by the High Seas Fleet under its Commander-in-Chief, Ingenohl.

Warrender saw Ingenohl's ships and closed, mistaking the High Seas Fleet for the smaller raiding force, while Ingenohl mistook the British force for Jellicoe's Grand Fleet of Battle. Ingenohl acted cautiously, ordering Hipper to proceed with his bombardment without apparently telling him of the British ships, while withdrawing the High Seas Fleet towards its bases. Warrender chased Ingenohl until he realized that the east coast ports to the north of his position were under attack, when he turned towards Hipper.

Meanwhile, eight pre-Dreadnoughts were sailed from Rosyth and the Grand Fleet from Scapa Flow, all three movements threatening to encircle Hipper: however, inept communications by the British allowed him to escape.

When the Germans attempted to repeat their successful raid on the east coast ports in January 1915 the British were pre-warned, again by intelligence, and better prepared. As a result Hipper's three battlecruisers were intercepted by Beatty's five battlecruisers at the Battle of Dogger Bank on January 24, the first direct clash between such ships.

Consequently the armoured cruiser *Blücher* was sunk and Hipper's flagship, the battlecruiser *Seydlitz*, was damaged, while on the British side Beatty's own flagship, *Lion*, was also badly damaged. Nevertheless Beatty transferred to *New Zealand* and continued his pursuit of the Germans until the threat of mines and U-boats caused him to break off the attack. Dogger Bank was a moral victory for the Royal Navy but not a decisive battle, although it made the German navy ever more cautious in its excursions into the North Sea.

One of the more memorable images of the war at sea is that of *Blücher* capsizing with her sides covered with men. *Blücher* was last in the German battle line formation, where she was repeatedly hit. At a range of 18,000m/20,000yds, a shell from *Princess Royal* penetrated her forward ammunition handling spaces causing a catastrophic fire. Beatty might have been able to do more damage to the other German ships but his fleet concentrated their fire on *Blücher* and allowed the other German vessels to escape, although *Seydlitz* was badly damaged and on fire. Like other German ships *Blücher* proved difficult to sink: a torpedo provided the *coup de grâce*.

TOP LEFT: The Indefatigable class of battlecruisers, one of which was *Australia*, bore the brunt of the North Sea actions. Often by the time squadrons of the Grand Fleet could deploy from Scapa Flow, the Germans had returned to harbour. TOP RIGHT: Returning from the bombardment of English east coast towns in January 1915, the armoured cruiser *Blücher* was caught by British forces and sank. ABOVE: *Derfflinger* was one of the three battlecruisers under the command of the German admiral Hipper.

The Battle of Jutland followed much the same theme, with a threatened raid intending to draw out the British fleet which would then be destroyed piecemeal. After Jutland the High Seas Fleet rarely left the Heligoland Bight, and there were few opportunities for the British Grand Fleet to come to grips with its enemy, while Beatty kept the Grand Fleet ready at Scapa Flow.

23

The Battle of Jutland

Jutland was the greatest battleship engagement of all time. On the outbreak of World War I most Royal Navy officers expected a decisive battle, *der Tag* (the day), between the battleships of the Grand Fleet, commanded by Admiral Jellicoe, and the German High Seas Fleet, commanded by Admiral von Pohl. However, German strategy was defensive, and on sweeps into the North Sea, the Germans avoided contact with the larger Grand Fleet. On the other hand, Beatty, in command of the British battlecruisers, adopted an aggressive strategy and at the Battles of the Heligoland Bight in December 1914 and of Dogger Bank in January 1915 the Germans were lucky to escape without serious losses.

However, when Admiral von Scheer replaced Pohl in command of the High Seas Fleet in January 1916, he prepared a strategy of attrition to counter the Royal Navy's distant blockade. He hoped to defeat the British by making hit-and-run raids on North Sea coastal towns that would bring the ships into battle piecemeal where they would be destroyed by minefields, submarines and local concentrations of superior numbers of German surface warships.

In May 1916 Scheer sent his battlecruisers out, under Admiral Hipper, hoping to draw Beatty's battlecruisers on to the High Seas Fleet. However, when British naval intelligence became aware of these plans, the Grand Fleet sailed from Scapa Flow as well as the battlecruisers from Rosyth.

TOP: **Close-up of the German battlecruiser *Seydlitz* on fire during the Battle of Jutland. Despite her after-turrets being burned out she reached Germany and was repaired.** ABOVE: **The British battleship *Warspite* flying three battle ensigns at about 18.00 during the "run to the north" on May 31, 1916. The German fleet is to the south-east.**

At 15.20 on May 31, 1916, the cruiser *Galatea* made the time-honoured signal "Enemy in sight" and Beatty turned his battlecruisers to the south-east to engage, opening fire at extreme range. As Beatty closed the range, *Indefatigable* and *Queen Mary* were hit and blew up and he uttered his infamous remark that there was "something wrong with our bloody ships today". Later it was thought that the British practice of achieving rapid fire by storing ready-use ammunition in exposed positions might have been the cause of losing these fine ships.

Beatty also lost contact with the supporting Fifth (Fast) Battle Squadron, and, after he had sighted the German High Seas Fleet, at 16.46 he turned towards Jellicoe, thus ending the first phase of the battle known as the run to the south.

At 17.33 Jellicoe and Beatty sighted each other's forces. Warned of the presence of the High Seas Fleet, Jellicoe now deployed the Grand Fleet into line of battle and crossed the head of the German line, but as he did so a third battlecruiser, *Invincible*, was hit and also blew up. At 18.33 Scheer ordered a simultaneous 16-point (180-degree) turn: to Jellicoe it seemed that the Germans had vanished in the haze. Twenty minutes later Scheer ordered another turn and again the head of his line came under fire, then at 19.18 he ordered a final 16-point turn.

Meanwhile Jellicoe, fearing a torpedo attack and unwilling to risk a night action, had made two alterations of course away from the Germans. Jellicoe was much criticized for this: had he taken greater risks at this stage of the battle, there is every possibility that he would have inflicted heavy casualties on the Germans.

As night fell the battlecruisers engaged each other, but during the night Scheer set course for Horns Reef while Jellicoe steered for the Ems River. There were plenty of skirmishes, but no one informed Jellicoe that Scheer was crossing behind him and by morning the seas were empty.

Jutland was a material and tactical victory for Scheer and the High Seas Fleet, and the Germans scored a propaganda victory too by the way they reported the battle first. However, it was a strategic victory for the Grand Fleet. While the Germans inflicted losses on the numerically superior Grand Fleet in the ratio of three to one, they had failed to break the British blockade or to wrest control of the North Sea from the Royal Navy.

On the other hand, the Royal Navy had failed to achieve the expected new Trafalgar, and the Navy and its public were bitterly disappointed. The German navy did not come out again until a mutiny and the armistice in 1918. Churchill summed affairs up when he said that Jellicoe was the only person who could have lost the war in an afternoon. The controversy about whether he could have done more continues to the present.

RIGHT: **John Jellicoe was Commander-in-Chief of the British Grand Fleet at the Battle of Jutland, the only man, Churchill said, who could have lost World War I in an afternoon.** FAR RIGHT: **Admiral Scheer commanded the German High Seas Fleet in 1916. His ships sank more than the British and his superior tactical handling of the fleet outwitted Jellicoe.** BELOW: **A German picture of the destruction of the British battlecruiser *Queen Mary* during the Battle of Jutland or Skagerrakschlacht at 16.26 on May 31, 1916. Beatty, when he saw his ships blowing up, asked if there was something wrong with the British ships.**

BRITISH LOSSES	GERMAN LOSSES
Battlecruisers	**Battlecruisers**
Indefatigable	None
Queen Mary	**Pre-Dreadnoughts**
Invincible	*Pommern*
Pre-Dreadnoughts	**Armoured Cruisers**
None	None
Armoured Cruisers	**Light Cruisers**
Black Prince	*Elbing*
Defence	*Frauenlob*
Warrior	*Rostock*
Light Cruisers	*Wiesbaden*
None	**Destroyers**
Destroyers	*S35*
Ardent	*V4*
Fortune	*V27*
Nestor	*V29*
Nomad	*V48*
Shark	**Crew Killed**
Sparrowhawk	2551
Tipperary	
Turbulent	
Crew Killed	
6097	

The scuttling at Scapa Flow

According to the terms of the armistice which brought about a temporary halt to the hostilities of World War I in continental Europe, Germany was obliged to have all her U-boats and about 70 surface warships interned, whose fate would then be decided by the treaty negotiations at Versailles.

When the German fleet steamed for the Firth of Forth they were met at sea by Beatty's Grand Fleet which had formed two parallel columns, comprising nearly 400 warships including 13 squadrons of battleships, battlecruisers and cruisers and the USN Sixth Battle Squadron. The Allied ships were at action stations even though their guns were trained fore and aft.

The German fleet arrived at the Firth of Forth on the morning of November 21. Beatty had no intention of treating this as merely an internment of the German navy, but was determined by stage management to make this an abject surrender, equivalent to major defeat in battle. The German navy was in an incipient state of mutiny, which Beatty dealt with by telling the plenipotentiaries of the Sailors' and Workers' Soviet of the North Sea command to "go to hell", and ordered that "the German flag will be hauled down at sunset and will not be hoisted again without permission".

Over the next few days the German ships were moved in groups to Scapa Flow, where they were all assembled by November 27. By mid-December 1918 the 20,000 crew members who had sailed the ships to Scapa Flow were reduced to maintenance crews of less than 5,000 officers and men, and in June 1919 these were further reduced to skeleton crews of less than 2,000.

TOP: *Seydlitz* leads the German battlecruisers into Scapa Flow on November 21, 1918. ABOVE: A close-up of the *Seydlitz* such as the British had not seen during the war. For four years the British Grand Fleet and the German High Seas Fleet had occupied each others' thoughts and actions. When they finally met, the British fleet was ready for action, though guns were trained fore and aft.

The armistice was extended several times while the treaty negotiations continued, in which, as far as the Royal Navy was concerned, the British were just as anxious to destroy the naval power of Germany as they were to prevent an increase in naval power of any other nation by the acquisition of the German ships. Finally it was agreed that all the interned ships should be surrendered and under the terms of the Treaty of Versailles Germany would only be allowed to keep six of her oldest pre-Dreadnought battleships of the Deutschland or Braunschweig classes, six light cruisers, 12 destroyers and no submarines.

LEFT: German battleship *Kaiser* taken from the air on November 21, 1918. BELOW LEFT: David Beatty, Jellicoe's successor as the Commander-in-Chief of the British Grand Fleet, caught open-mouthed as he watches the German High Seas Fleet entering an internment which he was determined to turn into surrender. BELOW: The wreck of the proud *Seydlitz* after she had been scuttled on June 21, 1919. The salvage of the German fleet took many years: the ships were raised and towed, mostly keel-up, to Scotland where they were broken up in the inter-war years. Some of the work was contracted out, so that by the 1930s there were German tugs, flying the Nazi's Swastika flag, engaged in towing the hulks between Scapa Flow and the Firth of Forth.

However, rather than allow the Royal Navy to seize his ships, Reuter, the German admiral at Scapa Flow, was making preparations to scuttle them. After he had read the details of the Treaty of Versailles in *The Times* newspaper, his only source of reliable intelligence, Reuter sent the cryptic message "Paragraph eleven. Confirm" on June 21, 1919, which was his order to scuttle the fleet. Although the British First Battle Cruiser Squadron immediately returned from exercises it was too late to prevent the German action.

Over 406,420 tonnes/400,000 tons of warships were sunk, including ten battleships (*Kaiser, Prinzregent Luitpold, Kaiserin, König Albert, Friedrich der Grosse, König, Grosser Kurfüst, Kronprinz Wilhelm, Markgraf,* and *Bayern*), and five battle-cruisers (*Seydlitz, Moltke, Von der Tann, Derfflinger* and *Hindenburg*), and also five cruisers and 31 other ships. Twenty-four other ships, including the battleship *Baden*, were beached by the British to prevent them from sinking. Officially the British were outraged and attempted to blame the government in Berlin for ordering the scuttling, but in private senior officers of

the Royal Navy were relieved that the German navy, once the second most powerful in the world, had been reduced to a minor status, and that the problem of what to do with the interned ships had been resolved. Perversely Admiral Scheer, the last commander-in-chief of the High Seas Fleet, took pride that the honour of the German navy had somehow been saved.

The remnants of the old Imperial German Navy became the Reichsmarine in April 1919 under the Weimar Republic and were given the task of defending the German Baltic coast against attacks by the Bolsheviks who were consolidating their grip on the Russian state. Salvage operations on the sunken ships at Scapa Flow lasted over the next two decades. It was an ignominious end to Germany's imperial and naval ambitions.

Directory of Battleships

There were very few fleet engagements after the Battle of Trafalgar in 1805, the most studied being the Battle of Tsushima in 1905 between the Japanese and Russians. The annihilation of the Russian fleet altered the balance of power in Europe, which coincided with the resurgence of the USN and the rise of the German navy. Germany had imperial ambitions and though its fleet was only intended for a limited purpose, German naval armament was perceived as a threat by Britain, then the greatest naval power in the world. A deadly arms race started across the North Sea which became a symptom, if not the cause, of World War I. In the event the German warships outside the North Sea were quickly rounded up, and though the Germans adopted tactics intended to defeat the Royal Navy by attrition, they never succeeded. Der Tag, the day when the two fleets would meet in decisive battle, was a disappointment to both sides although the Germans won materially, tactically, and in terms of propaganda. The Germans realized too late that submarine warfare was the only way that they could have won the war at sea.

LEFT: **The British built warships for navies throughout the world, although in war they frequently took them over for their own use. The Chilean *Almirante*, seen here, served in World War I as the British HMS *Canada*.**

Dreadnought

The change from the mixed calibres of previous designs to the all-big-gun armament, which Cuniberti had advocated and which Fisher adopted, was a direct result of increasing gun ranges and the need for a single calibre whose fall of shot could be distinguished by spotters.

British naval architects were already considering an all-big-gun design when Cuniberti's article was printed in English, and when Admiral Sir Jacky Fisher became First Sea Lord in October 1904 he tasked a committee to look at various arrangements of turrets. The USN had similar proposals under review and their analysis of the Battle of Tsushima would also convince the Japanese. Spotters needed to see the fall of shot in order to calculate range, but the gun range was increasing so much that the splashes of large- and medium-calibre guns could not be told apart. The obvious solution was to fit guns all of the same calibre.

Naval officers were also impressed by the economy of carrying only one outfit of ammunition and spares. However, the greatest improvement in *Dreadnought* was a result of the bold decision to fit four turbine-driven shafts. This was only four years after the Royal Navy had sent its first turbines to sea fitted in destroyers. The decision-making process was marked by Fisher's energy. The Committee on Design met on January 3, 1905, and by the end of February had made its

TOP: **HMS *Dreadnought*, which gave her name to the type she founded. In the background is Nelson's *Victory* and coming up the harbour are three submarines which were also part of Fisher's revolution.** ABOVE: ***Dreadnought*, again with *Victory* in the background, consciously linking the new great ship to the concept of the Royal Navy's supremacy at sea.**

recommendations. *Dreadnought* was laid down on Trafalgar Day, October 21, 1905, launched on February 10, 1906, and completed in December of the same year. This was something of a record even for the super-efficient Royal Dockyard of Portsmouth, although it was a little longer than the 12 months that Fisher claimed. Nevertheless, Fisher had energized everybody and everything and deserves much of the credit for her quick build.

Her naval architects deserve some credit, too. The decision to fit turbines instead of reciprocating engines saved space and about 1,016 tonnes/1,000 tons of weight and when this was combined with the hull form it allowed *Dreadnought* unprecedented speed, in excess of 20 knots. This had been rigorously tested in the model ship tanks at Haslar. Her sea trials were highly successful. The high forecastle kept *Dreadnought* dry, the wide beam to accommodate turrets on each side of the superstructure kept down the roll and the turbines reduced vibration. Consequently foreign navies immediately wanted to copy her. Nevertheless, the first German Dreadnoughts, the Westfalens, were not ready until 1909, and the first Japanese Dreadnoughts, *Satsuma* and *Aki,* and the first Americans, the South Carolina and Delaware classes, in 1910.

The designers made two mistakes, probably forced upon them by naval officers, among them the gunnery expert and future Commander-in-Chief of the Grand Fleet, John Jellicoe. The two wing turrets had limited arcs of fire; it would have been better to place an extra turret on the centre line and accept the increased weight penalty. As it was, fully loaded she was 3,556 tonnes/3,500 tons more than her designed displacement and *Dreadnought* sat so low that her armoured belt was under water and useless. Also, to provide a convenient support for a derrick to hoist her boats, the foremast with its gun-direction platform was placed aft of the fore funnel. This meant that if smoke or heat haze did not obscure the gun director then the acrid exhaust gases would choke the crew. These defects could not be rectified, although later she was armed with more light guns, her topmasts were cut down and she received a larger gun-direction platform and searchlight control positions.

Dreadnought saw the start of World War I as flagship of the Fourth Battle Squadron, until superseded by the more modern *Benbow*. On March 18, 1915, in the Pentland Firth, she became the first and only battleship to sink a submarine, the German *U-29*. In May 1916 she became flagship of the Third Battle Squadron of the Edward VII class ships at Sheerness, guarding the Thames, and so missed the Battle of Jutland, and on June 14, off Dunnet Head, *Dreadnought* attempted but failed to ram a second submarine. She returned to the Grand Fleet in 1918, was placed in reserve in 1919 and scrapped in 1922. *Dreadnought* was a singleton; she named not a class but a type of ship.

Dreadnought

Class: *Dreadnought.* Launched 1906
Dimensions: Length – 160.6m/527ft
 Beam – 25m/82ft
 Draught – 9.5m/31ft
Displacement: 18,400 tonnes/18,110 tons
Armament: Main – 10 x 305mm/12in guns
 Secondary – 24 x 12pdr guns and
 5 x 455mm/18in torpedoes
Machinery: 18 Babcock and Wilcox boilers,
 4 shafts, 17,375kW/23,300shp
Speed: 21 knots
Complement: 695 men

Bellerophon class

This class was very similar to the *Dreadnought* and the ships were also built very rapidly. Internally the propulsion machinery was the same, but they were also fitted with an inner longitudinal bulkhead designed to localize damage from a torpedo hit, known as a torpedo bulkhead. The tripod foremast was placed over the bridge superstructure and thus clear of funnel gases, but a second tripod mainmast was added with a "fighting top" which was exposed to the fumes of both funnels. While these two masts gave the Bellerophons a more balanced look than *Dreadnought*, the fire control position on the mainmast proved useless and was removed along with the topmasts during the war.

The secondary armament was also improved from 12-pounders (75mm/3in) to 100mm/4in guns. Initially some guns were sited on the main turrets' roofs, but these were later placed in casemates in the superstructure. Other changes during World War I included the removal of torpedo nets and the after torpedo tube, more extensive radio aerials, searchlight platforms, additional anti-aircraft guns,

and funnel caps. By 1918 all three ships had ramps on the A and Y turrets and could fly off either a Sopwith Pup fighter biplane or a Sopwith Strutter reconnaissance aeroplane.

Bellerophon joined the Home Fleet in 1909 and the Fourth Battle Squadron of the Grand Fleet in August 1914, and fought at the Battle of Jutland. Her career was remarkable for two collisions, one with *Inflexible* at Portland in 1911 and one with a merchantman in 1914. She was placed in reserve at the war's end and broken up in 1921.

Superb was flagship of the Fourth Battle Squadron at Jutland. In November 1918 she led the Allied Fleet through the Dardanelles, was paid off in 1919, briefly

TOP: *Bellerophon* underway. The design fault of placing the foremast behind the funnel has been corrected. *Bellerophon*'s jack, not normally flown at sea, appears to indicate she is dressed for some occasion. ABOVE: *Superb* in the Hamoaze at Plymouth. BELOW: *Temeraire* in Plymouth Sound.

a target and broken up in 1921. *Temeraire* followed a similar career, but was used as a seagoing training ship until being scrapped in 1921–2. The war service of these ships proved the soundness of the basic Dreadnought design.

Bellerophon class

Class: *Bellerophon, Superb, Temeraire.*
  Launched 1907
Dimensions: Length – 160.3m/526ft
  Beam – 25.2m/82ft 6in
  Draught – 8.3m/27ft 3in
Displacement: 19,100 tonnes/18,800 tons
Armament: Main – 10 x 305mm/12in guns
  Secondary – 16 x 100mm/4in guns and
  3 x 455mm/18in torpedoes
Machinery: 18 boilers, 4 shafts,
  17,151kW/23,000shp
Speed: 21 knots
Complement: 733 men

St Vincent class

The third class of ships of the basic Dreadnought design followed a trend of gradual improvement and increase in size. Horsepower was increased to offset the rise in displacement and the hull form began to be refined, so the St Vincents were slightly slimmer and longer. As in the Bellerophons the after fire-control position proved useless and was later removed.

A new 305mm/12in gun was introduced with a longer barrel, although this did not prove effective as the higher muzzle velocity shortened the barrel life and reduced accuracy at longer ranges. Pre-war modifications included lowering the topmasts and moving the secondary armament from the main gun roofs. Wartime modifications were similar to the Bellerophons with the addition of funnel caps, searchlight towers and aircraft ramps.

St Vincent was commissioned into the Home Fleet as flagship in 1910, fought at the Battle of Jutland as part of the First Battle Squadron, and was broken up.

The future King George VI served as a Lieutenant on *Collingwood* at Jutland. Later this class moved from the First to the Fourth Battle Squadron. *Collingwood* was sold for scrap in 1922. *Vanguard* followed her sisters into the Home and Grand Fleets and Jutland, and between them these ships fired over 250 305mm/ 12in rounds at the German High Sea Fleet, and received no hits. On July 9, 1917, *Vanguard* suffered a violent explosion and sank with appalling speed, killing 804 men. This was later attributed to faulty ammunition.

In this period a number of ships blew up when not in action. Although sometimes attributed to sabotage or other covert enemy action, the cause was invariably the spontaneous combustion of ammunition.

BELOW: ***Vanguard*** **(with other Dreadnoughts beyond her) approaching Portsmouth.** RIGHT: ***Vanguard* followed by another St Vincent class. The artist A. B. Cull has captured the winter weather when these ships operated in the North Sea.**

St Vincent class

Class: *St Vincent, Collingwood, Vanguard.* Launched 1908–9

Dimensions: Length – 163.4m/536ft
Beam – 25.7m/84ft 2in
Draught – 7.9m/25ft 11in

Displacement: 19,875 tonnes/19,560 tons

Armament: Main – 10 x 305mm/12in guns
Secondary – 20 x 100mm/4in guns and
3 x 455mm/18in torpedoes

Machinery: 18 boilers, 4 shafts,
18,270kW/24,500shp

Speed: 21 knots

Complement: 718 men

Invincible, Indomitable and *Inflexible*

One of Fisher's more debatable ideas concerned the armoured cruiser. Fisher wanted a cruiser that was larger and faster than any other cruiser, which could protect trade by hunting down and destroying every other smaller cruiser and could also act either as a heavy scout in pursuit of an enemy or as support of the van of the battlefleet. In official words: "To engage the enemy battlecruisers in a fleet action, or, if none are present, by using their speed to cross the bow of the enemy and engage the van of his battlefleet".

The result was the battlecrusier (so named in 1913) of which the Invincibles were the first. They were long ships so that they could accommodate the number of boilers needed to give them their high speed, and like *Dreadnought* they mounted a uniform large-calibre armament. However, when compared to the battleships they were lightly armoured although externally they looked very similar. Like *Dreadnought* they had twin rudders and four turbine-driven shafts which made them very effective. They were however vulnerable not just against battleships but also against ships of their own type firing large-calibre guns. In the case of the Invincibles the wing turrets, P and Q, had very limited-beam firing arcs. Later in the war *Indomitable* was fitted with flying-off ramps over these turrets.

At the Battle of Jutland the Fifth Battle Squadron had been loaned to the Battlecruiser Fleet and the Invincibles, who formed the Third Battlecruiser Squadron, had been lent to the Grand Fleet. Inevitably Jellicoe placed the three battlecruisers in the line of battle, where they suffered accordingly. Although

Invincible and *Indomitable* disabled the *Wiesbaden* and *Pillau* and hit *Lützow*, when *Invincible* came under sustained fire from the German battleships *Derfflinger, Lützow* and *König*, a shell hit Q turret causing a huge explosion that blew her in half. There were only six survivors from a crew of over 1,000.

Previously *Invincible* had taken part in the first naval engagement of the war, the Battle of Heligoland Bight on August 28, 1914. In November 1914 she had been ordered to sail from Devonport still with dockyard labourers onboard to hunt for Admiral Graf von Spee's squadron in the South Atlantic. On December 8, 1914, she had fought at the Battle of the Falkland Islands, when *Invincible, Inflexible* and their consorts sank the German *Scharnhorst* and *Gneisenau*, the light cruisers *Leipzig* and *Nürnberg*, and two colliers. During the battle *Invincible* was hit 22 times by smaller-calibre shells, but without fatalities.

As a new ship *Inflexible* visited New York in 1909. At the outbreak of World War I she was flagship of the British Mediterranean Fleet and with *Indomitable*, in August 1914, was involved in the unsuccessful hunt for the German battlecruisers *Goeben* and *Breslau*. She joined *Invincible* in the hunt for *Graf Spee* and the Battle of the Falkland Islands. In February and March 1915 she wore out her guns' barrels during bombardments in the Dardanelles, where she was flagship of the British Dardanelles Squadron. On March 18, 1915, *Inflexible* was hit nine times by Turkish batteries and ran on to a mine, needing to be beached for temporary repairs before

going to Malta for full repairs. At the Battle of Jutland she fired 88 305mm/12in rounds and received no damage herself. On August 19, 1916, *Inflexible* was attacked unsuccessfully by the German submarine *U-65*, and on January 31, 1918, she collided with a British submarine in the ironically named Battle of May Island. She was sold for scrap in 1921.

On commissioning *Indomitable* carried the Prince of Wales on a visit to Canada. At the outbreak of World War I she took part in the chase of the *Goeben* and *Breslau*, and in November 1914 participated in a preliminary bombardment of the Dardanelles forts that may have alerted the Turks to future British and allied intentions. She joined the Second Battlecruiser Squadron and fought at the Battle of Dogger Bank on January 25, 1915. There she fired on *Blücher*, closing the range to 5,490m/6,000yd, and received no damage herself. Afterwards *Indomitable* towed *Lion* back to Rosyth. At the Battle of Jutland *Indomitable* fired 175 305mm/12in rounds, hitting *Derrflinger* (three times), *Seydlitz* (once) and the pre-Dreadnought *Pommern*. She was sold for scrap in 1921.

OPPOSITE AND ABOVE: *Invincible* and her sisters were conceived as fast armoured cruisers, but inevitably in the case of ships with an armament of 305mm/12in guns fleet commanders wanted to place them in the line of battle and they were restyled battlecruisers. The lack of fire control equipment clearly indicates that the heavy guns had outranged the means of laying them accurately – especially in the frequent mists and fogs of the North Sea.

BELOW: **The fine photograph of a previous *Inflexible*, taken from the ramparts of the fortress of Malta, shows how far warship design had evolved since the masted turret ship *Inflexible* of 1874–1903.**

Invincible, Indomitable and Inflexible

Class: *Invincible, Indomitable, Inflexible.*
Launched 1907
Dimensions: Length – 172.8m/567ft
Beam – 23.9m/78ft 6in
Draught – 8m/26ft 2in
Displacement: 17,652 tonnes/17,373 tons
Armament: Main – 8 x 305mm/12in guns
Secondary – 16 x 100mm/4in guns and
5 x 455mm/18in torpedoes
Machinery: 31 boilers, 4 shafts,
30,574kW/41,000shp
Speed: 26 knots
Complement: 784 men

LEFT: *Neptune* at anchor and working her boats. She is wearing the flag of the Commander-in-Chief, Home Fleet. ABOVE: *Neptune* at anchor in the fleet anchorage of Scapa Flow during World War I. Note that the after tripod mast and flying bridges have been removed. BELOW LEFT: A period picture postcard showing *Hercules* dressed overall while underway. The Royal Navy was fond of reusing the famous names of its ships, and chose the classic names of earlier wooden-walled battleships, like *Hercules*, to remind the world that Britainnia ruled the waves.

Neptune, Colossus and Hercules

When the American and the Argentine navies built Dreadnoughts which would fire 10 and 12 guns on the broadside, the British staggered their midships turrets, on a longer hull, so that both midships turrets could be fired across the deck. To leave the boats clear and open the firing arcs, a flying bridge was introduced linking the islands of the superstructure.

The roof-mounted 100mm/4in guns were suppressed and placed in the superstructure behind armoured shields. Pre-war a searchlight platform was added, the after control position was removed, the fore funnel heightened and a clinker cowl fitted.

Neptune was the fastest British battleship to date, making nearly 23 knots on trials. She fought at Jutland, where she suffered no damage, and was broken up in 1919. *Colossus* and *Hercules*, the last two 305mm/12in-gunned battleships of the period, were half-sisters to *Neptune*.

Realizing that in battle the wreckage from the flying bridges would fall on P and Q turrets, this was reduced in size, and in 1917 removed completely. The after control position was never fitted but, in a retrograde step, the forward mast and control position were placed abaft the fore funnel. In *Colossus* the 100mm/4in guns in the superstructure were protected by dropping ports; *Hercules* had shields. Pre-war the fore funnel was raised and later the torpedo nets were removed.

Colossus was hit at Jutland by two shells, the only Grand Fleet battleship at Jutland to be damaged. In 1919–20 she was painted in Victorian black, white and buff livery and served as a training ship at Devonport for cadets. She was broken up in 1928. *Hercules* also fought at Jutland. In November 1918 she carried the Allied Naval Commission to Kiel, and was sold for breaking up in 1921.

Neptune

Class: *Neptune.*
　Launched 1909
Dimensions: Length – 166.42m/546ft
　Beam – 25.9m/85ft
　Draught – 8.7m/28ft 6in
Displacement: 19,996 tonnes/19,680 tons
Armament: Main – 10 x 305mm/12in guns
　Secondary – 16 x 100mm/4in guns and
　3 x 455mm/18in torpedoes
Machinery: 18 Yarrow boilers, 4 shafts,
　18,643kW/25,000shp
Speed: 21 knots
Complement: 759 men

Colossus and Hercules

Class: *Colossus, Hercules.*
　Launched 1910
Dimensions: Length – 166.4m/546ft
　Beam – 25.9m/85ft
　Draught – 8.8m/28ft 9in
Displacement: 20,550 tonnes/20,225 tons
Armament: Main – 10 x 305mm/12in guns
　Secondary – 16 x 100mm/4in guns and 3 x
　535m/21in torpedoes
Machinery: 18 boilers, 4 shafts,
　18,643kW/25,000shp
Speed: 21 knots
Complement: 755 men

Indefatigable class

As successions of Dreadnought-type battleships and battlecruisers were built year on year, their design improved. However this class has been criticized because *Indefatigable* was a near replica of *Invincible,* which had been laid down three years before. *Australia* and *New Zealand* were laid down at the same time as the Lion class battlecruisers, which incorporated all the lessons learned so far, were bigger by 8,128 tonnes/8,000 tons, more heavily armed (340mm/13.5in guns) and better armoured (230mm/9in on the belt), matching the increases in equivalent ships being built in Germany. There is no direct evidence why this should be so, other than speculation that it was done on grounds of dockyard capacity, speed, cost (£1.7 million – *Australia* and *New Zealand* were paid for by their namesake countries) or to produce a second homogeneous division of battleships.

The class were some 6m/20ft longer than *Invincible,* which allowed greater staggering and better arcs of fire to the midships turrets, P and Q. The fore funnel was increased in height to help clear smoke from the bridge and the after control position was initially fitted but soon dismantled. Various light guns were added during the war, and after Jutland, *Australia* and *New Zealand* were given an additional 25mm/1in of armour between P and Q turrets. They also received searchlights, range clocks, and, in 1918, flying-off platforms over the midships turrets. These two ships already differed from *Indefatigable* in their internal arrangement of armour and their bridge layouts, and had 745.7kW/1,000shp more power.

Indefatigable served in the British Mediterranean Fleet and took part in the unsuccessful chase of *Goeben* and *Breslau*. In November 1914 she bombarded Cape Helles in the Dardanelles, before joining the Second Battlecruiser Squadron. At the Battle of Jutland *Indefatigable* was hit by *Von der Tann*. Two rounds entered the after (X) magazine, causing an explosion,

ABOVE: *Indefatigable* **was one of three similar battlecruisers. Fast but lightly armoured, she was hit by** *Von der Tann* **at the Battle of Jutland and blew up. The fundamental weakness of these ships was their lack of armour, but some ships had laid great emphasis on rapid rate of fire (rather than accuracy).**

and as *Indefatigable* veered out of line a second salvo hit her forward and she blew up.

Indefatigable class

Class: *Indefatigable, Australia, New Zealand.*
  Launched 1909–11
Dimensions: Length – 179.8m/590ft
  Beam – 24.4m/80ft
  Draught – 7.9m/26ft
Displacement: 18,800 tonnes/18,500 tons
Armament: Main – 8 x 305mm/12in guns
  Secondary – 16 x 100mm/4in guns and
  3 x 455mm/18in torpedoes
Machinery: 32 boilers, 4 shafts,
  32,811kW/44,000shp
Speed: 25 knots
Complement: 800 men

Australia

At the start of World War I the Admiralty in London and the government in Canberra struggled over *Australia*'s deployment. The Australian government wanted *Australia* as a deterrent and defence against a raid by the German East Asiatic Squadron, yet was anxious to strike its own blow in the war. Therefore after mustering the Australian fleet in Sydney, *Australia* escorted Australian and New Zealand troops for the capture of the German colonies of Samoa and New Guinea.

In September 1914 *Australia* steamed east to Fiji. Japan had declared war on Germany and *Australia* was sent to join Japanese ships off California which were intended to prevent the Germans using the Panama Canal. When the news came of the Battle of the Falklands, *Australia* was sent to join the British Grand Fleet at Scapa Flow; as she was too long for the Panama Canal she made passage via Cape Horn in late December 1914.

In the South Atlantic she sank the German merchantman *Eleonore Woermann*, thus ending enemy coaling arrangements. She was made flagship of the Second Battlecruiser Squadron, although following a collision with her sister ship *New Zealand* she missed the Battle of Jutland. Between January 1915 and November 1919 *Australia* steamed some 91,565km/56,908 miles, mostly on the Northern Patrol, the distant blockade of Germany. She became the first aircraft-carrying ship of the Australian navy, using a platform built over the guns from which Sopwith fighters were launched as scouts and to attack Zeppelins.

After her return to Australia in May 1919, she once more became flagship of the Royal Australian Navy and played a leading role in the visit of the Prince of Wales in another battlecruiser, the British *Renown*. However, *Australia* consumed too much of the navy's budget and manpower, and by 1920 she was

ABOVE: *Australia*, **paid for and manned by Australians, played an active part in World War I and became a source of pride for the new nation.**
BELOW: **Following the Washington naval treaty, *Australia* was de-equipped and scuttled in April 1924 off Sydney.**

downgraded to a drill ship at Flinders Naval Depot with a secondary role as a fixed defensive battery. In November 1921 she was paid off into reserve.

Australia was included in the tonnage allowed the British Empire under the terms of the Washington Treaty. There were efforts to have her preserved as a monument, but she was stripped, and in April 1924 towed to sea, where the pride of the Australian navy was scuttled, amid much public lament – the battlecruiser *Australia* had been a symbol of the country's burgeoning nationhood.

Australia

Class: *Indefatigable, Australia, New Zealand.*
Launched 1909–11
Dimensions: Length – 179.8m/590ft
Beam – 24.4m/80ft
Draught – 7.9m/26ft
Displacement: 18,800 tonnes/18,500 tons
Armament: Main – 8 x 305mm/12in guns
Secondary – 16 x 100mm/4in guns and
3 x 455mm/18in torpedoes
Machinery: 32 boilers, 4 shafts,
32,811kW/44,000shp
Speed: 25 knots
Complement: 800 men

New Zealand

In 1909 the Prime Minister of New Zealand decided to set an example to the other British Dominions by offering to fund a "first class battleship" for the Royal Navy. In the event New Zealand paid for an Indefatigable class battlecruiser and a sister ship to *Australia*, which was rather cheaper than the super-Dreadnoughts which were being introduced.

The British Admiralty sent *New Zealand* on a tour of the Dominions in 1913 to show them what could be done, before sending her to join the First Battlecruiser Squadron of the Grand Fleet. There she took part in the Battles of Heligoland Bight and Dogger Bank, and when Beatty's own flagship *Lion* was damaged at Dogger Bank, he transferred his flag to *New Zealand*.

In April 1916 *New Zealand* and *Australia* collided in fog in the North Sea. *New Zealand* was repaired just in time to rejoin the fleet before the Battle of Jutland, but *Australia* missed the great battle. As if to make up for this *New Zealand* fired more rounds at Jutland than any other ship in the battle – a total of 420 305mm/12in shells. In turn she was hit just once by a shell which landed on X turret without major damage or casualties.

In November 1917 *New Zealand* also fought in the Second Battle of Heligoland Bight. Unlike *Australia*, who was manned largely by Australians, there were mostly British and very few New Zealanders in the battlecruiser *New Zealand*. Nevertheless her captain had been presented with a Maori battledress and

it was thought to be unlucky if he did not wear this when going into battle.

In 1919–20 Admiral Jellicoe was sent on a world tour to assess the Empire's needs for defence – the British Admiralty still hankered after an Empire navy and Jellicoe was supposed to report what contributions the Dominions could make. He chose *New Zealand* as his flagship and she was specially modified to provide him with suitable office and living accommodation. It has been reckoned that nearly one-third of the population of her home country saw the battlecruiser *New Zealand* while she was in New Zealanad waters. *New Zealand* was scrapped in 1923.

ABOVE: *New Zealand* became Jellicoe's flagship for his 1919 mission to advise on the naval requirements of the British Empire. The photograph shows his specially built quarters on the port side forward of the funnels. ABOVE RIGHT: *New Zealand* bows-on showing the fine lines of this class of ship. LEFT: Visitors' day on *New Zealand*. Although only a handful of the ship's company were in fact New Zealanders, the population of New Zealand took a proprietary interest in the affairs of their ship, and her captain was expected to wear Maori costume when going into action.

New Zealand

Class: *Indefatigable, Australia, New Zealand.*
   Launched 1909–11
Dimensions: Length – 179.8m/590ft
   Beam – 24.4m/80ft
   Draught – 7.9m/26ft
Displacement: 18,800 tonnes/18,500 tons
Armament: Main – 8 x 305mm/12in guns
   Secondary – 16 x 100mm/4in guns and
   3 x 455mm/18in torpedoes
Machinery: 32 boilers, 4 shafts,
   32,811kW/44,000shp
Speed: 25 knots
Complement: 800 men

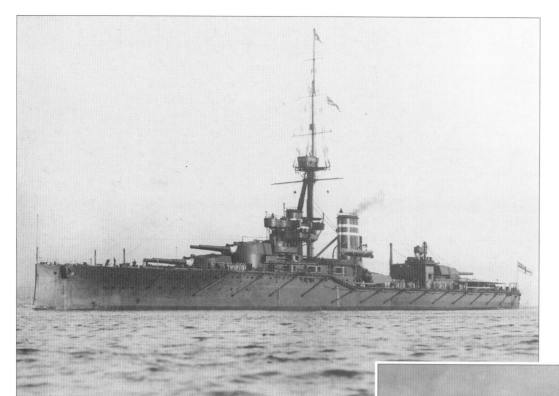

LEFT: **Port bow photograph of one of the Orion class. For some extraordinary reason the foremast has been put back behind the funnel where the gunnery control optics, and their operators, will be affected by the smoke and haze.** BELOW: **A starboard profile of this class of ship, showing the hot fumes which must have made climbing the foremast a noxious experience. Producing four Dreadnoughts a year was about the industrial capacity of Great Britain.**

Orion class

The 305mm/12in, 50-calibre gun had proved inaccurate and caused too much barrel wear, so the 340mm/13.5in gun, not seen since the 1890s, was reintroduced in the Orion class. The lower muzzle velocity and larger shell was successful in reducing instability in flight and increased accuracy, and, with increased elevation of firing, the 340mm/13.5in gun could hit a target at 21,950m/24,000yd. The shell when it arrived was also considerably heavier (635kg/1,400lb) than the 305mm/12in version (567kg/1,250lb).

The Orions incorporated many minor improvements. The awkward arrangement of placing guns midships to fire athwartships was abandoned and all were mounted on the centre line. The forward turrets, A and B, and the after ones, X and Y, were super-firing. On the other hand, blast through the sighting hoods of the lower turrets prevented these guns being fired ahead. Side armour was extended up to the main deck, overcoming the problem that at full load the armoured belt tended to be submerged and therefore useless. The mainmast was reduced to a small pole

mast. Bilge keels were fitted to reduce roll.

Once more the foremast and its control position were placed aft of the fore funnel, and the only reason for this can be a continued emphasis on seamanship (the need for a derrick to hoist boats) over gunnery. However, the interference this caused with optics and the hazard to health was much reduced because the funnel served fewer boilers.

When *Thunderer* was fitted with the Scott director aiming system in 1912 and took part in a competitive shoot against *Orion* she scored many more hits.

During World War I the topmasts were reduced and torpedo nets removed, the fire-control platform extended, plating over magazines increased and flying-off platforms fitted over B turret. *Thunderer* had an additional runway over X turret.

Monarch rammed *Conqueror* in December 1914, damaging her bows, and *Revenge* collided with *Orion* causing similar damage. These four ships formed the Second Battle Squadron at the Battle

of Jutland, where they fired 198 rounds but neither caused nor sustained any damage. Discarded after the Washington Treaty, *Thunderer* survived until 1926 as a cadet training ship, then, like her sisters in 1922, was broken up.

Orion class

Class: *Orion, Conqueror, Monarch, Thunderer.*
Launched 1910–11
Dimensions: Length – 177.1m/581ft
Beam – 27m/88ft 6in
Draught – 7.3m/24ft 1in
Displacement: 22,560 tonnes/22,200 tons
Armament: Main – 10 x 340mm/13.5in guns
Secondary – 16 x 100mm/4in guns and
3 x 535mm/21in torpedoes
Machinery: 18 boilers, 4 shafts,
20,134kW/27,000shp
Speed: 21 knots
Complement: 752 men

Lion class

The Lion class battlecruisers were 6 knots faster than the Orion class battleships. To achieve this they had 42 rather than 18 boilers, and were 36.6m/120ft longer. To reduce weight the maximum thickness of armour was reduced from 305mm/12in to 230mm/9in and the super-firing after turret was removed. Nevertheless, the displacement increased by over 4,064 tonnes/4,000 tons to 22,556 tonnes/22,200 tons.

They were handsome ships, known in the fleet as the "Cats", and were the subject of much favourable comment inspired by the Admiralty, which encouraged rumours exaggerating their speed and armoured strength.

When launched *Lion* had the foremast placed between the closely spaced first and second funnels, but the heat was so intense that the crew in the gun-direction platform were stranded. The direction platform was re-sited forward of the fore funnel on a pole mast and this was reinforced by struts, turning it into a tripod.

Lion was Admiral Beatty's flagship in the Battle Cruiser Force. She took part in the Battles of Heligoland Bight, Dogger Bank and Jutland. At Dogger Bank she fired nearly 250 rounds but made only four hits; one on *Blücher*, one on *Derfflinger* and two on *Seydlitz*. In turn she was hit by 16 280mm/11in and 305mm/12in rounds and had to be towed back by *Indefatigable*. She was also damaged at Jutland, and saved from explosion by the heroism of one man who ordered the flooding of a magazine. Q turret was temporarily removed in late 1916. She made numerous other sorties, but was scrapped in 1924.

Princess Royal fought at the Battle of Heligoland Bight before escorting the first Canadian troops across the Atlantic in September 1914, and guarding the North America and West Indies station during the hunt for Admiral Graf von Spee's squadron. She was also in action at Dogger Bank. At Jutland she was hit by *Derfflinger, Markgraf* and *Posen*, but although suffering damage, casualties and on fire, she remained in action. *Princess Royal* was part of the covering force during the Second Battle of Heligoland Bight on November 17, 1917. She was sold for scrap in 1922.

Lion class

Class: *Lion, Princess Royal.*
Launched 1910–11
Dimensions: Length – 213.4m/700ft
Beam – 27m/88ft 6in
Draught – 8.4m/27ft 8in
Displacement: 26,690 tonnes/26,270 tons
Armament: Main – 8 x 340mm/13.5in guns
Secondary – 16 x 100mm/4in guns and
2 x 535mm/21in torpedoes
Machinery: 42 boilers, 4 shafts,
52,199kW/70,000shp
Speed: 27 knots
Complement: 997 men

ABOVE: *Lion*, flagship of Admiral Sir David Beatty's First Battlecruiser Squadron, leads *Princess Royal* to sea and into action on May 31, 1916. LEFT: *Lion* being towed into Armstrong's yard at Newcastle upon Tyne for repairs after the Battle of Jutland. BELOW: The Lion class were graceful ships well equipped with radio, which Beatty did not seem to want to use at Jutland and so lost control of the Fifth Battle Squadron that was allocated to him.

Queen Mary and Tiger

Superficially similar to the Lion class, Queen Mary incorporated several minor improvements. An additional 3,729kW/5,000shp gave her half a knot extra speed, the armoured belt was modified, and the larger main armament shell gave even greater stability in flight and accuracy, though for a period she could shoot at greater ranges than the guns could be sighted. Wartime modifications included a larger bridge and gun-direction platform with director control in 1915, reduced topmasts, and additional legs for the foremast.

Queen Mary was at the Battle of Heligoland Bight but missed the fighting at Dogger Bank. At Jutland she was another ship of the Battle Cruiser Force which came under fire from the German Derfflinger. She had fired about 150 rounds at Seydlitz when she was hit on Q turret and shortly afterwards between A and B turrets. The forward magazines exploded and the fore part of the ship disappeared and as she settled, listing to port, a further enormous explosion occurred, barely half an hour after the battle had started.

BELOW: Queen Mary and Tiger were at first glance the same as the Lion class, but they were half a knot faster and bigger-gunned. BOTTOM: Tiger with Renown beyond her, steaming at full speed into a heavy swell in the North Sea (1917 or 1918). Together, Lion, Tiger, Princess Royal and Queen Mary were known as the Cats.

The Tiger class were half-sisters to Lion and Princess Royal, together known as the Cats. Externally the difference was the rearrangement of the turrets, Q turret now being placed aft of three equally spaced funnels. For the first time in a British battlecruiser, the secondary armament consisted of 150mm/6in guns. Internally, improved boilers gave Tiger 63,385kW/85,000shp, but the speed increase this enabled was disappointing while the fuel consumption increased alarmingly. Protection (230mm/9in maximum armour) was just as poor as in other battlecruisers.

At the Battle of Dogger Bank, Tiger exchanged fire with German opponents, and was hit by six large-calibre hits. At Jutland, she was hit 15 times without her ammunition exploding, thus seemingly proving that in ships where the rules of handling ammunition were followed there was less risk of disaster.

Queen Mary

Class: Queen Mary. Launched 1912
Dimensions: Length – 214.4m/703ft 6in
  Beam – 27.1m/89ft
  Draught – 8.5m/28ft
Displacement: 27,200 tonnes/26,770 tons
Armament: Main – 8 x 340mm/13.5in guns
  Secondary – 16 x 100mm/4in guns and
  2 x 535mm/21in torpedoes
Machinery: 42 boilers, 4 shafts,
  55,928kW/75,000shp
Speed: 27.5 knots
Complement: 997 men

Tiger

Class: Tiger. Launched 1913
Dimensions: Length – 214.6m/704ft
  Beam – 27.6m/90ft 6in
  Draught – 8.7m/28ft 6in
Displacement: 28,885 tonnes/28,430 tons
Armament: Main – 8 x 340mm/13.5in guns
  Secondary – 12 x 150mm/6in guns and
  4 x 535mm/21in torpedoes
Machinery: 39 boilers, 4 shafts,
  63,385kW/85,000shp
Speed: 29 knots
Complement: 1,121 men

LEFT: **The four ships of this class formed the newest squadrons of Dreadnought, until** *Audacious* **was sunk by a mine off Northern Ireland in October 1914.** BELOW: *King George V* **lying under a huge crane at Portsmouth and being fitted out after launch. The crane is being used to begin to assemble** *King George V*'s **355mm/14in guns.**

King George V class

This class was similar to the Orions, but with the foremast placed forward of the funnels and modified during World War I, including the fitting of flying-off ramps in 1918. Almost the last of the Dreadnoughts to be built before the outbreak of war, the King George V class was the epitome of the type.

King George V served the war in the Grand Fleet and became a post-war gunnery training ship. She was finally scrapped in 1926 (under the terms of the Washington Treaty) when *Nelson* and *Rodney* were completed.

Ajax served the war in the Grand Fleet and operated in the Black Sea against Russian revolutionaries in 1919. She was scrapped in 1926. *Centurion* also served the war in the Grand Fleet and after operations in the Black Sea was converted to a radio-controlled target ship. She was used as a decoy in World War II and then sunk as a block ship off Normandy in France on June 9, 1944.

In October 1914 the converted German liner *Berlin* laid a minefield off Malin Head on the north coast of Ireland, where the British Grand Fleet was using Loch Swilly as a base whilst the anti-submarine defences of Scapa Flow were being improved. On the morning of October 27, 1914, as she steamed out

on exercises with the other super-Dreadnoughts *Centurion, Ajax, King George V, Orion, Monarch* and *Thunderer*, the *Audacious* struck a mine on her port side amidships, quickly developed a list and lost power. Most of her crew were taken onboard the White Star liner *Olympic*. *Audacious* slowly settled by the stern and, at nightfall, after the rest of her crew had been rescued, she capsized, there was an explosion, and she sank.

No lives were lost, and the sinking was blamed on the weakness of the longitudinal bulkheads which were buckled in the initial explosion and had allowed floodwater to spread, though it seems that the damage control procedures in the ship could not have been very proficient.

Ludicrously, since the incident had been witnessed by American passengers onboard *Olympic*, the Commander-in-Chief of the Grand Fleet, Jellicoe, persuaded the British Admiralty to try to keep the sinking a secret. While everyone but the British acknowledged the loss, the British kept *Audacious* in the Navy List and reticence on the subject damaged British credibility. *Audacious* was the first loss of a major warship in World War I.

King George V class

Class: *King George V, Centurion, Audacious, Ajax.*
  Launched 1911–12
Dimensions: Length – 182.1m/597ft 6in
  Beam – 27.1m/89ft
  Draught – 8.7m/28ft 8in
Displacement: 23,370 tonnes/23,000 tons
Armament: Main – 10 x 340mm/13.5 guns.
  Secondary – 16 x 100mm/4in guns and 2 x
  535mm/21in torpedoes
Machinery: 18 boilers, 4 shafts,
  23,117kW/31,000shp
Speed: 21 knots
Complement: 782 men
Former name of *King George V* was *Royal George*

Iron Duke class

Similar in many respects to the King George V class, the Iron Dukes were 7.7m/25ft longer and 0.3m/1ft wider in the beam. However they were 2,032 tonnes/2,000 tons heavier, mainly because of the increase in the secondary armament from 100mm/4in to 150mm/6in to meet the greater ranges at which torpedo-boats could fire their improved weapons. A large direction platform was fitted on build, and these were also the first battleships to be fitted with anti-aircraft guns – two 12pdr on the after superstructure of *Iron Duke* in 1914. The stern torpedo tubes which had been a feature of design until now were suppressed.

The secondary armament casemates were, however, a problem: the hinged plates that closed off the revolving turrets were vulnerable in any kind of seaway and once washed away or damaged allowed seawater to flood on to the mess decks. The problem was solved by fitting dwarf bulkheads and rubber seals, but the design fault was that the guns were mounted too low in the hull. After Jutland searchlights and increased armour were fitted.

Iron Duke was flagship of the Home Fleet under Admiral Callaghan, and then of the Grand Fleet, under both Jellicoe and Beatty. In 1919–26 she was part of the British Mediterranean Fleet, and bombarded Red Army positions in the Black Sea in support of the White Russians during operations there in 1919–20. While the others of her class were scrapped under the terms of the Washington Treaty, *Iron Duke* was retained in a demilitarized state as a training and depot ship. Demilitarization included removal of B and Y turrets, and

BELOW: *Iron Duke* in 1914 as flagship of the Grand Fleet under Admiral Sir John Jellicoe. *Iron Duke* served on into World War II when she was an accommodation ship at Scapa Flow.

a substantial part of her armour, and limiting her speed, through the removal of boilers, to 18 knots. *Iron Duke* spent World War II at Scapa Flow, with the rest of her armament removed, was damaged by bombs in 1939 and finally sold for scrap in 1946. *Benbow* served her time in the Grand Fleet, joined the British Mediterranean Fleet between 1919 and 1926 and, like others of her class, provided gunfire support for White Russians in the Black Sea in 1919–20, and was sold for scrap in 1931. *Emperor of India*, whose former name was *Delhi*, spent World War I in the Grand Fleet (but missed Jutland because she was in refit), and was in the Mediterranean between 1919 and 1926. She was sunk as a gunnery target in 1931.

Between them the Iron Dukes fired 292 rounds of 340mm/ 13.5in ammunition during Jutland, of which *Marlborough* fired 162. She was torpedoed amidships and a hole 21m x 6m/70ft x 20ft was blown in her side, abreast the boiler rooms, where she was only protected by coal bunkers. Unlike *Audacious* she was able to keep station at 17 knots and did not cease firing until her guns were prevented from bearing by her list. She made her way to the Humber, and after three months' repairs on the Tyne she rejoined the Grand Fleet. *Marlborough* served with the rest of her class in the Mediterranean until 1926, then the Atlantic Fleet until 1929, and was scrapped in 1932.

TOP: *Iron Duke* enters Portsmouth. On the left is *Queen Elizabeth* and on the right is *Victory*. All three ships are flying the St George cross signifying an Admiral in command. ABOVE LEFT: *Emperor of India*, showing how with a following wind the bridge and in particular the gunnery direction platform could be enveloped in smoke and funnel gases. ABOVE: An over-flight of biplanes portends the coming struggle between the surface ship and the aircraft.

Iron Duke class

Class: *Iron Duke, Marlborough, Emperor of India, Benbow*. Launched 1912–13

Dimensions: Length – 189.8m/622ft 9in
Beam – 27.4m/90ft
Draught – 8.8m/29ft

Displacement: 25,400 tonnes/25,000 tons

Armament: Main – 10 x 340mm/13.5in guns
Secondary – 12 x 150mm/6in guns and
4 x 535mm/21in torpedoes

Machinery: 18 boilers, 4 shafts,
21,625kW/29,000shp

Speed: 21 knots

Complement: 995 men

Queen Elizabeth class

Though armed and armoured as battleships, the Queen Elizabeth class was fast enough to operate with the Battle Cruiser Force, to which, as the Fifth (Fast) Battle Squadron, they were attached during the Battle of Jutland (except *Queen Elizabeth* herself who was in dockyard hands). They were regarded as the finest battleships of their era. Their 380mm/ 15in guns were one reason for this and another – which her crew appreciated – was that with oil-fired boilers they were cleaner and more spacious than coal-fired ships. The six 380mm/15in guns could deliver a heavier broadside than any five-turret predecessor, and the guns were more accurate and suffered less barrel wear than the 340mm/13.5in. To secure supplies of oil the British government bought shares in Middle Eastern oil companies, thus inadvertently setting the course of foreign policy later in the century.

All five ships were overweight when completed and in practical terms their speed was about 24 knots.

Like other Dreadnoughts they were modified after Jutland and were fitted with range clocks and deflector scales, searchlight towers and additional deck armour. In 1918 all five were fitted with flying-off ramps on B and X turrets.

Although the handling of the Fifth Battle Squadron at Jutland was severely criticized, its participation in the Battle Cruiser Force probably saved Beatty's ships from an even worse mauling. In particular, the Germans were impressed by the accuracy of *Valiant*'s shooting.

Built at Portsmouth, but towed to Fairfield's to be fitted with her engines, as first of class *Queen Elizabeth* had a stern walk and two additional 150mm/6in guns under the quarterdeck, but these were removed in 1915 when they proved wet. Instead single guns with stern arcs were retrofitted port and starboard underneath X turret, as was done in the rest of the class.

TOP: *Queen Elizabeth*, after she had been modernized in the interwar years. The forward tripod had been replaced by a heavy control tower. ABOVE: In peacetime ceremonial duties were part of life on a battleship and here, on *Queen Elizabeth*, seamen and Royal Marines man the side for HM the King, and prepare to salute him in the traditional manner by giving him three cheers.

Queen Elizabeth bombarded forts in the Dardanelles in early 1915, but was recalled to the Grand Fleet although she missed the Battle of Jutland. In 1917, after Beatty had become Commander-in-Chief of the Grand Fleet, he took her for his flagship. Briefly in September 1917 she wore the flag of Admiral Mayo USN. The surrender of the German High Seas

LEFT: **Rough weather when the deck would be out of bounds.** BELOW: **In calm weather the forecastle was a place of work and here *Queen Elizabeth*'s crew are seen preparing to launch paravanes (used to keep mines clear of striking the hull).**

Fleet was signed onboard *Queen Elizabeth* on November 15, 1918. Refitted and then modernized, she served on into World War II.

Repaired after a collision with *Barham* on December 2, 1915, *Warspite* was ready in time for the Battle of Jutland. She fired over 250 rounds, but was hit herself by some 15 305mm/12in rounds. At a critical moment her steering gear failed and *Warspite* steamed a full circle under the German gunfire but the Grand Fleet came up to drive off the Germans before she could be destroyed, and she limped back to Rosyth. Her repairs were just completed when on August 24 she was damaged in another collision, this time with *Valiant*. *Warspite* was partially modernized in 1924–6 and served in World War II.

The Federated States of Malaya paid for a fifth ship, named *Malaya*. She was ready in time for Jutland where she fired 215 rounds and was hit herself eight times by 305mm/12in rounds. *Malaya* visited Cherbourg for celebrations of the peace in April 1919 and in 1920 visited Germany. In 1921 *Malaya* took Prince Arthur of Connaught to India and on to Malaya. She served in the fleet until 1948.

Valiant served with the Grand Fleet throughout World War I and fired 299 rounds at the Battle of Jutland, receiving only slight splinter damage. She was modernized in 1929–30 and rebuilt in 1937–9.

Barham was named after Lord Barham, First Lord of the Admiralty and architect of the Campaign of Trafalgar in 1803–5. In the fighting at Jutland, *Barham* fired 337 rounds and during the "run to the north" came under heavy fire from the German High Seas Fleet. Midshipman Blackett, who subsequently became one of the greatest scientists of the 20th century and winner of the Nobel Prize for Physics in 1948, described this as "our five minutes' hate". It really lasted much longer and was extraordinarily unpleasant. It is estimated that some 500 305mm/12in bricks were fired at the *Barham* and the

rest of the squadron. "How we survived with so very few hits I have no idea," Blackett said. "Everyone was very relieved that the Grand Fleet had joined up, for it was exceedingly unpleasant alone."

Like her sisters, *Barham* was modernized from 1931–4, emerging with a single smokestack, enhanced protection against long-range plunging gunfire, and additional anti-aircraft guns, as well as a hangar and catapult for two seaplanes.

In World War II, *Barham* was capsized and blew up after she had been torpedoed by a German U-boat in the Mediterranean. The U-boat was returning from a special forces operation in North Africa when it found itself in the path of the British Mediterranean Fleet making a sortie to the west. The U-boat commander was lucky to get in his snapshot and it hit *Barham* with three torpedoes. The loss of *Barham* was recorded on film and makes for poignant viewing, as well as unique footage.

Queen Elizabeth class

Class: *Queen Elizabeth, Warspite, Valiant, Barham, Malaya.* Launched 1913–15
Dimensions: Length – 196.6m/645ft
 Beam – 27.7m/91ft
 Draught – 9.5m/31ft
Displacement: 27,940 tonnes/27,500 tons
Armament: Main – 8 x 380mm/15in guns
 Secondary – 14 x 150mm/6in guns and
 4 x 535mm/21in torpedoes
Machinery: 24 boilers, 4 shafts,
 41,759kW/56,000shp
Speed: 25 knots
Complement: 925 men
A sixth ship, to be named *Agincourt*, was cancelled. All ships of the class were extensively rebuilt between the wars, and their anti-aircraft armament improved.

Royal Sovereign class

Although known as the Royal Sovereigns, the British Admiralty referred to these ships as the Revenge class, and in fact *Ramillies* was the first ship to be laid down. Compared to the Queen Elizabeths their speed was reduced to 21 knots, and the 150mm/6in guns placed further aft to keep them drier. The obvious visual difference was the single, large, centrally placed funnel.

Ramillies was built with 2.1m/7ft-wide bulges faired into the hull to absorb the effect of an exploding torpedo. Filled with wood, tubes, oil and water, the bulges weighed an extra 2,540 tonnes/ 2,500 tons, but did not affect speed or fuel consumption, and were retrofitted in others of the class.

Up to this point all Dreadnoughts had had four shafts and twin rudders, but in this class two in-line rudders were fitted, the smaller, forward rudder intended to reduce vulnerability and make hand-steering, in an emergency, easier. In practice, the ancillary rudder proved ineffective and was removed.

When Fisher returned to office in 1914, he had the designs changed from mixed coal and oil to all oil-fired, with the intention of raising the horsepower and

with this the speed to 23 knots. He also had work on three other ships of this class, *Renown*, *Repulse* and *Resistance*, suspended as he wanted to replace them with battlecruisers.

After Jutland pumping and flooding arrangements were extended to cope better with damage, extra armour was placed over the magazines, and flash-tight doors on ammunition routes improved. Searchlight towers, range clocks and deflection scales were also fitted. By 1918 all ships had flying-off ramps over B and X turrets.

Only *Royal Oak* and *Revenge* fought at Jutland. The *Royal Sovereign* was completed in time, but missed the battle through engine problems. *Ramillies*'s completion was delayed after she had damaged her rudder on launch, and she did not join the Grand Fleet until 1917. *Resolution* was completed too late.

Royal Oak was torpedoed by the German U-boat *U-47* at Scapa Flow in 1939. *Royal Sovereign* was transferred to the Soviet Navy in 1944, and renamed *Archangelsk*, to be returned in 1949 when she was broken up. All others survived World Wars I and II and were sold for breaking up in 1948.

ABOVE: **The Royal Sovereign class of ships saw much active service in both World Wars of the 20th century, but were already slow ships when completed.** BELOW: *Revenge* **on a spring cruise in 1934. The effect of the Atlantic swell, even on a 28,450-tonne/28,000-ton battleship, would have been the same whatever the year, even though architects tried to build their ships for North Atlantic conditions.**

Royal Sovereign class

Class: *Ramillies, Resolution, Revenge (ex Renown), Royal Oak, Royal Sovereign.* Launched 1914–16
Dimensions: Length – 190.3m/624ft 3in
  Beam – 27m/88ft 6in
  Draught – 8.7m/28ft 6in
Displacement: 28,450 tonnes/28,000 tons
Armament: Main – 8 x 380mm/15in guns
  Secondary – 4 x 150mm/6in guns and
  4 x 535mm/21in torpedoes
Machinery: 18 boilers, 4 shafts,
  29,830kW/40,000shp
Speed: 21 knots
Complement: 937 men

Erin

The main concern of the Turkish navy in the run-up to World War I was superiority in the Aegean over its former vassal, Greece, and in the Black Sea over its traditional enemy, Russia. To meet these perceived threats, Turkey had ordered several ships in Britain including the new-build super-Dreadnought *Reshadieh*, and *Sultan Osman I* was purchased from Brazil while still in the yard. In addition to two cruisers and four destroyers, none of which were delivered, these ships were paid for in part by public subscription in Turkey. Resentment at their requisition in August 1914 by the Royal Navy, after the crews had arrived to steam them home, helped to bring Turkey into the war on the side

of Germany. As a result the Turkish navy was commanded by a German admiral on the side of the central powers.

Reshadieh (formerly *Reshad V*), renamed *Erin* in the Royal Navy, had the same gun plan as *Orion* and mixed elements of the King George V and Iron Duke class designs, but was slightly shorter and broader. Her extra beam meant that she could not fit into any Royal Navy dry dock and she had to be docked in private yards. She carried a main armament of ten 340mm/13.5in guns in twin turrets in the same layout but her secondary armament consisted of 150mm/6in guns. Her armour was equivalent to her British contemporaries, though she was regarded as rather

Erin	
Class: *Erin.* Launched 1913	
Dimensions: Length – 170.5m/559ft 6in Beam – 27.9m/91ft 7in Draught – 8.7m/28ft 5in	
Displacement: 23,150 tonnes/22,780 tons	
Armament: Main – 10 x 340mm/13.5in guns Secondary – 16 x 150mm/6in guns and 4 x 535mm/21in torpedoes	
Machinery: 15 boilers, 4 shafts, 19,761kW/26,500shp	
Speed: 21 knots	
Complement: 1,070 men	
A second ship of the class, *Reshad-i-Hammiss*, was cancelled.	

overcrowded and cramped for accommodation. She was readily recognized by her unusual reverse tripod mast, round funnels, and by Q turret being one deck higher than in her contemporary British designs. *Erin* was given improved fire-control equipment in 1917 and, in 1918, flying-off platforms on B and Q turrets. It is said that Japan's first battlecruiser, *Kongo,* also laid down in 1911 at Vickers, was derived from this design by Sir George Thurston.

Erin spent the war, including the Battle of Jutland, in the Grand Fleet. She was placed in reserve in 1919 and sold to the breakers in 1922, in the era when many ships were culled.

ABOVE: **The Royal Navy's requisitioning of a Turkish battleship which had been partly paid for by public subscription by the Turkish nation, and whose Turkish crew had already been formed, caused much resentment. This helped bring Turkey into the war on the side of Germany.** RIGHT: *Erin* **had a short career. Launched in 1913, she was broken up in 1922. The British Admiralty had a preference for large ships of similar types and equipment-fits:** *Erin* **had too many unique features to make her economic to retain.**

Agincourt

The battleship *Rio de Janeiro* was ordered by the Brazilian Government in November 1910 and she would have been the ultimate expression of the naval arms race between the Argentine, Brazil and Chile. She was to have been the most powerful warship not just in South America, but in the world, and she was for a time certainly the longest. However she was also a long time building as the Brazilians could not agree amongst themselves what armament to give their ships: various designs were considered between eight 405mm/16in and 14 305mm/12in guns, and eventually the latter was chosen, partly on the grounds of standardization of ammunition stock within the Brazilian fleet and partly under the influence of German advisers who were content with their own 305mm/12in guns. In the meantime Brazil's position in the arms race was costing 25 per cent of the national budget, which became untenable when the price of rubber collapsed and with it the Brazilian economy. In December 1913 *Rio de Janeiro* was sold to Turkey and renamed *Sultan Osman I*. Work recommenced and now included some luxury fittings.

The Turkish Government expected delivery of their new super-Dreadnought in July 1914, and her crew had arrived to take her, and *Reshadieh,* home, but as the delivery time neared Armstrong's were approached by the Admiralty to delay the

ABOVE: *Agincourt* was also destined for the Turkish navy but forcibly taken over by the Royal Navy. The picture on this page shows her as modified for British service, and opposite shows her with the flying bridges and tripod masts with which she was built.

handover of the ship. Then on July 31, 1914, with war imminent, the First Lord of the Admiralty, Winston Churchill, minuted that "Messrs Armstrong should be informed that in view of the present circumstances the Government cannot permit the ship to be handed over to a Foreign Power or to be commissioned as a public ship of a Foreign Government, or to leave their jurisdiction". Next day a company of Sherwood Foresters with fixed bayonets boarded the *Sultan Osman I* and escorted all the Turkish naval personnel off the ship. Money for the new ship had been raised partly by public subscription in Turkey, and her seizure by Britain strengthened the hand of the pro-German faction in the Turkish government. Two months later Turkey was at war with Britain.

Renamed *Agincourt*, her luxurious fittings gave her the nickname of "The Gin Palace" in the Royal Navy and appropriately her first captain and the core of her first crew came from the Royal Yacht. There were individual cabins for the officers and spacious accommodation for the crew but this

had been achieved by eliminating many watertight bulkheads. Like *Erin*, the armoured protection (maximum thickness 230mm/ 9in) was not up to Royal Navy standards (305mm/12in). The flying bridges – also known as "Marble Arches" – were no longer a feature of British designs and these, along with the tripod mainmast, were removed. To complete her eccentricity the seven turrets were named after the days of the week, Sunday, Monday, Tuesday, Wednesday, Thursday, Friday and Saturday. So unique was *Agincourt's* appearance that it became common to give stationing orders relative to her.

She was not a success in the Royal Navy: much of her equipment was non-standard and required more frequent visits to the dockyard. The 305mm/12in gun had not been fitted since the Indefatigable battlecruisers, and the single-lever loading arrangements were unusual. Besides concern for control of flooding if torpedoed, it was rumoured that she would break her back or turn turtle if she fired her full broadside.

Nevertheless, at the Battle of Jutland *Agincourt* was one of the first battleships to sight the German High Seas Fleet, and the sight of her 14 guns firing broadsides and enveloping her in a sheet of flame was described as awe-inspiring.

During the war the gunnery direction platform and bridge were enlarged, and searchlight towers around the second funnel were added, together with some extra, light guns.

After the war *Agincourt* was offered for sale to the Brazilian Government, which was not interested; Brazil's challenge to the first navies of the world had ebbed. *Agincourt* was converted to oil-fired boilers and given additional protection, and five turrets (Tuesday to Saturday) were removed so she could be used as a depot ship. However, these plans were dropped and she was scrapped in 1922, along with a great many other ships.

TOP: **As built, originally for the Brazilian government who sold her to the Turks, *Agincourt* had a prominent midships Sampson mast and two tripods.**

ABOVE: **Much of her equipment was, literally, foreign to the Royal Navy but such a powerful ship could not be allowed to go overseas into another navy. Subsequently her career in the Royal Navy was foreshortened.**

Agincourt

Class: *Agincourt.* Launched 1913
Dimensions: Length – 204.7m/671ft 6in
    Beam – 27.1m/89ft
    Draught – 8.2m/27ft
Displacement: 27,940 tonnes/27,500 tons
Armament: Main – 14 x 305mm/12in guns
    Secondary – 20 x 150mm/6in, 10 x 75mm/3in
    guns and 3 x 535mm/21in torpedoes
Machinery: 22 boilers, 4 shafts,
    25,354kW/34,000shp
Speed: 22 knots
Complement: 1,115 men

Canada

There is good evidence that during the period running up to World War I the British Admiralty used ships being built in British yards for foreign navies as a reserve. The Chilean Government had ordered two battleships as their response to the South American arms race, to be named *Almirante Latorre* and *Almirante Cochrane*. Turkish battleships being built in Britain had been seized, but Chile was a friendly country where there were large British business

BELOW: **Unlike Turkey whose ships, which were being completed in Britain, were requisitioned, Chile sold her two incomplete battleships to the Royal Navy.**

interests, and she was an important supplier of nitrates for the ammunition industry. As a result *Almirante Latorre* was purchased, though the hint to the Chilean Government that it should follow Australia, Malaysia and New Zealand in paying for a battleship did not work.

Canada was similar to the British Iron Dukes, but 12.2m/40ft longer and 2–3 knots faster, her funnels were taller and thicker, and she had a pole mainmast. In 1918 she had flying-off ramps on B and X turrets. *Canada* joined the Grand Fleet and fought at Jutland and in 1920 she was returned to Chile. In 1914 *Canada*'s sister ship *Almirante Cochrane* had been built up to the

forecastle deck, and in 1918 she was taken in hand and completed as the aircraft carrier *Eagle*.

Canada

Class: *Canada*. Launched 1913
Dimensions: Length – 201.5m/661ft
  Beam – 28m/92ft
  Draught – 8.8m/29ft
Displacement: 29,060 tonnes/28,600 tons
Armament: Main – 10 x 355mm/14in guns
  Secondary – 16 x 150mm/6in guns and
  4 x 535mm/21in torpedoes
Machinery: 21 boilers, 4 shafts,
  27,591kW/37,000shp
Speed: 23 knots
Complement: 1,167 men

LEFT: **The battlecruiser *Renown* was a familiar site off the coast in 1937.**
ABOVE: ***Renown*'s guns had a range of just over 32km/20 miles. Her rate of fire was about one round per minute and it was claimed that each shell could penetrate up to 1.46m/57in of wrought iron.**
BELOW: **All needs were catered for – large galleys and dining rooms, crowded messes and, on most warships, quiet places such as *Renown*'s chapel, seen here.**

Renown class

The Royal Navy had decided against building more battlecruisers when Fisher returned to office as First Sea Lord. He drew lessons from the Battle of the Falklands and to those who said that World War I would be over within a year, he promised to build his new ships quickly enough to participate. Using the material assembled for two Royal Sovereign class ships, Fisher ordered instead two fast battleships. They were 61m/200ft longer and 10,160 tonnes/10,000 tons heavier than previous battlecruisers, and armed with 380mm/15in guns instead of 305mm/12in, but they suffered from the same basic weakness of the battlecruiser concept in that they were too lightly armoured. However they were fast ships, reaching 30 knots, although not their designed speed of 32 knots.

They were also under-gunned on secondary armament. Under Fisher's influence 100mm/4in guns were selected, which even in triple mountings could not deliver the necessary weight of shells, and needed a disproportionately large crew.

Further, they were not delivered until after the weaknesses of the battlecruisers became tragically evident at the Battle of Jutland. Jellicoe, while still Commander-in-Chief of the Grand Fleet, proposed that both ships should be given increased armour as well as other post-Jutland modifications typical of the British Dreadnought fleet. The architects still could not solve the smoke problem and so the fore funnel was also raised 1.8m/6ft to clear the bridge of funnel gases.

At the end of the war they received more armour again. After World War I both ships were extensively refitted and in the inter-war years they were rebuilt, adding another 6,095 tonnes/6,000 tons.

Neither ship saw much action during World War I, although both led busy lives in the inter-war years and also fought in World War II.

Renown class

Class: *Renown, Repulse.* Launched 1916
Dimensions: Length – 242m/794ft
    Beam – 27.4m/90ft
    Draught – 7.8m/25ft 6in
Displacement: 28,095 tonnes/27,650 tons
Armament: Main – 6 x 380mm/15in guns
    Secondary – 17 x 100mm/4in guns and
    2 x 535mm/21in torpedoes
Machinery: 42 boilers, 4 shafts,
    83,518kW/112,000shp
Speed: 30 knots
Complement: 967 men

Courageous, Glorious and Furious

Fisher's ill-defined plans to "Copenhagen" the German fleet by forcing an entry into the Baltic gave rise to two extremes of his battlecruiser concept. *Courageous* and *Glorious* were thinly armoured, shallow draught, and fast. The hull was so light that on trials *Courageous* suffered buckling between the breakwater and the forward turret and both ships were strengthened. Fisher hoped to fit a 455mm/18in gun but it was not ready in time. Reckoned by some to be "white elephants", they were tried in a number of different roles. They were fitted with additional torpedoes (although there was no recorded incident of a contemporary Dreadnought successfully firing her torpedoes) and *Courageous* was briefly equipped as a minelayer. A significant advance was made in using small-tube boilers for the first time and double-helical turbines. With 18 Yarrow small-tube boilers they could achieve almost the same horsepower as the Renowns with 42 large-tube boilers.

Courageous and *Glorious* took part in an action against German light cruisers in November 1917. Both were converted to aircraft carriers in the 1920s.

BELOW: ***Courageous**, seen here alongside at Devonport, and **Glorious** were light battlecruisers in which even armament was sacrificed for speed. Eventually both ships were converted to aircraft carriers.*

Furious was similar in size to *Courageous* and *Glorious*, even down to her turret rings, but she had, at last, the 455mm/18in gun in single mountings. She was also slightly beamier. However while nearing completion she was converted to an aircraft carrier. Contrary to popular history, the Admiralty was very air-minded, appreciating the value of aircraft both for reconnaissance and as fighters – particularly after the Royal Naval Air Service's success in shooting down airships. Nearly all battleships were converted to carry flying-off ramps, and the decision was taken to platform over the whole of *Furious*'s forecastle, and suppress the forward turret as one large flying-off ramp. There was space for a hangar under the ramp. Derricks were fitted for hoisting seaplanes onboard, but trials showed that an aircraft like the Sopwith Pup could also be landed on the deck.

The conversion was a limited success and in August 1917 *Furious* was taken in hand for a rebuild which would turn her into a through-deck carrier. The Royal Navy is sometimes accused of being too battleship-minded in the inter-war years and criticized for not paying enough attention to naval aviation, but up to April 1, 1918 (when the RAF was formed), it owned one of the largest air forces in the world and the loss of so many men and machines to the RAF was a serious setback.

TOP: **Another view of *Courageous*, this time from the quarter.** ABOVE: ***Furious* also was converted to an aircraft carrier (above left) on board where in the inter-war years the Royal Navy experimented with the first arrester wires (above right). Despite the loss of expertise by the transfer of large numbers of aircraft and airmen to the RAF, the Royal Navy continued to innovate and, despite a lack of modern aircraft, maintained its tactical skill in the use of aircraft. Control of the Fleet Air Arm did not revert to the Royal Navy until just before World War II. Nevertheless, the Fleet Air Arm newly restored to the Admiralty's operational control made rapid progress and distinguished itself well in all theatres of the war, against the German, Italian and Japanese navies.**

Courageous class

Class: *Courageous, Glorious.* Launched 1916
Dimensions: Length – 239.7m/786ft 3in
    Beam – 24.7m/81ft
    Draught – 7.1m/23ft 4in
Displacement: 19,540 tonnes/19,230 tons
Armament: Main – 4 x 380mm/15in guns
    Secondary – 18 x 100mm/4in guns and
    2 x 535mm/21in torpedoes
Machinery: 18 small-tube boilers, 4 shafts,
    67,113kW/90,000shp
Speed: 32 knots
Complement: 828 men

Furious

Class: *Furious.* Launched 1916
Dimensions: Length – 239.7m/786ft 6in
    Beam – 26.8m/88ft
    Draught – 6.4m/21ft
Displacement: 19,826 tonnes/19,513 tons
Armament: Main – 2 x 455mm/18in guns
    Secondary – 11 x 140mm/5.5in guns and
    2 x 535mm/21in torpedoes
Machinery: 18 boilers, 4 shafts,
    67,113kW/90,000shp
Speed: 31 knots
Complement: 880 men

LEFT: *Michigan* at anchor at evening colours. The low light through the lattice masts shows their delicate and elaborate construction. ABOVE: *Michigan* firing a broadside of her 305mm/12in guns during 1912. BELOW: The larger navies were beginning to experiment with replenishment at sea, but operations like this coaling while underway from the bunker ship *Cyclops* to *South Carolina* in 1914 were slow and cumbersome.

South Carolina class

The launch of the British *Dreadnought* with her size, turbine machinery, speed of 21 knots, and main battery of ten 305mm/12in guns shook naval observers everywhere. The USN had already ordered its first all-big-gun ships, but the design was artificially constrained by the US Congress to 16,257 tonnes/ 16,000 tons, and delayed while the USN absorbed the lessons of the Great White Fleet and of the Battle of Tsushima. In the end, *South Carolina* and *Michigan* were similar to earlier US pre-Dreadnoughts, including in the retention of reciprocating engines.

They did, however, have two novel features: lattice masts and super-firing guns. Apparently the original intention had been to install a gun-direction platform amidships on a flying bridge, but this was dropped in favour of the lattice or cage mast. Experiments had shown that this stood up well to shellfire and reduced vibration at the top of the mast and certainly the gun-direction platform could be carried up higher. This did not always work and in 1918 a heavy gale bent *Michigan*'s mast over. Nevertheless, the lattice mast was retro-fitted into many US pre-Dreadnoughts

and became the distinctive recognition mark of future US battleships.

The other novel feature was the super-firing turret. This enabled the full complement of main armament guns to be brought to bear on either beam, giving ships arranged like this a superiority over other Dreadnoughts with guns arranged in echelon or staggered in midships positions. The super-firing gun soon became the norm in every other navy.

South Carolina visited Europe in 1910–11, took part in US interventions in Haiti and Mexico in 1913–14, and spent the rest of World War I on the east coast of the USA. In 1919 she made four round-trips to France, bringing home over 4,000 servicemen, and was scrapped in 1924.

Michigan visited England and France in 1910, and spent the rest of her career in the Atlantic. In spring 1914 she was involved in the Vera Cruz incident when many of her crew served ashore. In World War I she stayed in the western Atlantic, but between January and April 1919 she brought home more than a thousand veterans of the western front. She was scrapped in 1924.

South Carolina class

Class: *South Carolina, Michigan.* Launched 1908
Dimensions: Length – 137.2m/450ft
   Beam – 24.5m/80ft 5in
   Draught – 7.5m/24ft 7in
Displacement: 16,260 tonnes/16,000 tons
Armament: Main – 8 x 305mm/12in guns
   Secondary – 22 x 75mm/3in guns and
   2 x 535mm/21in torpedoes
Machinery: 12 boilers, 2 shafts.
   11,304kW/16,500ihp
Speed: 18.5 knots
Complement: 869 men

LEFT: Quite soon the USN Dreadnoughts like the Delaware class did away with wing turrets and mounted all turrets on the centre line.

Delaware class

The Delaware class, reckoned to be the first true Dreadnoughts in the USN, were 25 per cent larger than the previous class, capable of over 20 knots, and their ten centre-line 305mm/12in guns exceeded anything so far built. The secondary armament consisted of 125mm/5in guns, which became the standard size in the USN.

Absorbing more lessons from the Battle of Tsushima, large but fully enclosed conning towers were intended to reduce the exposure of bridge personnel. *Delaware* was fitted with triple-expansion reciprocating engines, while *North Dakota* was turbine-driven. The reciprocating engine proved more efficient and reliable and – the Americans claimed – *Delaware* was the first ship that could steam for 20 hours at full speed without a breakdown. *North Dakota*'s first turbines proved inefficient and better, geared turbines were installed in 1915 delivering 23,340kW/31,300shp.

Delaware class

Class: *Delaware, North Dakota*. Launched 1909
Dimensions: Length – 155.5m/510ft
  Beam – 26m/85ft 4in
  Draught – 8.3m/27ft 3in
Displacement: 20,707 tonnes/20,380 tons
Armament: Main – 10 x 305mm/12in guns
  Secondary – 15 x 125mm/5in guns and
  2 x 535mm/21in torpedoes
Machinery: 14 boilers, 2 shafts,
  18,640kW/25,000shp
Speed: 21 knots
Complement: 933 men

Delaware served with the British Grand Fleet in the US Sixth Battle Squadron, and was scrapped in 1924. *North Dakota* was reduced to an auxiliary role after World War I and lasted until 1931.

Florida class

LEFT: *Florida*'s after turrets trained out to starboard and ready for action: the men do not appear to be wearing any kind of action clothing and the awning will have to be taken down to prevent blast from the guns from tearing it apart.

Compared to the Delaware class, these ships had an improved 125mm/5in gun with better armour and, once the US Congressional limit had been breached, showed the tendency for US Dreadnoughts to grow in size. Both ships landed seamen and marines during the Vera Cruz crisis in 1914. *Florida* joined the British Grand Fleet at Scapa Flow, and in December 1918 she escorted President Wilson to France and was at New York for the Victory Fleet Review. *Utah* was based in Ireland to cover Allied convoys as they approached Europe. Both ships were modernized in the 1920s when they received bulges, new oil-fired boilers and the funnels were trucked into one. The lattice mainmast was removed and an aircraft catapult fitted over the midships turret. Under the 1930 London Naval Treaty, *Florida* was scrapped and *Utah* was converted to a radio-controlled target ship in 1931. On December 7, 1941, *Utah* was hit by two aerial torpedoes and capsized in the attack on Pearl Harbor, where her wreck can still be seen.

Florida class

Class: *Florida, Utah*. Launched 1909–10
Dimensions: Length – 155.5m/510ft
  Beam – 27m/88ft 3in
  Draught – 8.6m/28ft 3in
Displacement: 22,175 tonnes/21,825 tons
Armament: Main – 10 x 305mm/12in guns
  Secondary – 16 x 125mm/5in guns and
  2 x 535mm/21in torpedoes
Machinery: 12 boilers, 4 shafts,
  20,880kW/28,000shp
Speed: 21 knots
Complement: 1,001 men
Beam increased to 32m/106ft by the addition of
anti-torpedo bulges.

LEFT: The outline of USN Dreadnoughts did not change much until some of them were modernized in the 1920s. Here *Wyoming*, taken about 1937, can be compared with ships on the previous page. The most obvious feature is that a pole mast replaces the after cage mast and there is a single funnel.

Wyoming class

Class: *Wyoming, Arkansas.* Launched 1911
Dimensions: Length – 165.8m/544ft
    Beam – 28.4m/93ft 2in
    Draught – 8.7m/28ft 7in
Displacement: 26,420 tonnes/26,000 tons
Armament: Main – 12 x 305mm/12in guns
    Secondary – 21 x 125mm/5in guns and
    2 x 535mm/21in torpedoes
Machinery: 12 boilers, 4 shafts,
    20,880kW/28,000shp
Speed: 21 knots
Complement: 1,063 men

Twenty per cent larger again than their predecessors, the Wyomings had two more 305mm/12in guns, and the secondary armament was carried one deck higher. Both ships operated with the British Grand Fleet during World War I and afterwards in the Atlantic and Pacific. After modernization in 1925–7 they emerged with broader beams and thicker deck armour, and their silhouettes changed by single funnels, a pole mainmast and an aircraft catapult.

In 1931 *Wyoming* became a training ship, losing first her armour and six of the main turrets, and, in 1944 when the priority became anti-aircraft training, gaining extra 125mm/5in guns. She was scrapped in 1947.

Arkansas was also used for pre-World War II training, and she supported the occupation of Iceland and escorted convoys in the North Atlantic until refitted in 1942. Emerging with a tripod foremast, she was used for shore bombardment in support of the Normandy landings and off Southern France in 1944. Between February and May 1945, she supported the landings on Iwo Jima and Okinawa. *Arkansas* was expended during atomic bomb tests at Bikini Island in 1946.

New York class

LEFT: **A second modernization in the 1930s gave these and similar ships two tripod masts and a single funnel. The primary career of both ships was inshore bombardment.**

supported the Iwo Jima and Okinawa landings in 1945. *New York* was exposed during atomic bomb tests at Bikini Island and in 1948 was sunk as a target off Pearl Harbor. *Texas* is preserved as a memorial at San Jacinto and is the only remaining World War I-era US battleship still in existence.

Class: *New York, Texas.* Launched 1912
Dimensions: Length – 172.2m/565ft
    Beam – 29.1m/95ft 6in
    Draught – 8.7m/28ft 6in
Displacement: 27,433 tonnes/27,000 tons
Armament: Main – 10 x 355mm/14in guns
    Secondary – 21 x 125mm/5in guns and
    4 x 535mm/21in torpedoes
Machinery: 14 boilers, 2 shafts,
    20,954kW/28,100shp
Speed: 21 knots
Complement: 1,026 men

The two New Yorks with their 355mm/14in guns were last in the line of the original US Dreadnoughts. Both ships served with the British Grand Fleet in 1917–18. They were modernized in the 1920s, and became the first USN battleships to have tripod masts. However, oil-fired boilers, a single trunked funnel, additional deck armour and anti-torpedo bulges increased beam and displacement, so that they could no longer make 20 knots. They served throughout World War II, covering convoys in the North Atlantic and supporting the landings in North Africa in November 1942. *Texas* also bombarded targets off Normandy and Southern France in 1944. In the Pacific they

LEFT: *Oklahoma* passing Alcatraz in the 1930s. BELOW: Sailors swabbing out the 355mm/14in guns. The need for this function did not change with the passing of time. BOTTOM LEFT: *Nevada* operating a kite balloon off Cuba in World War I. BOTTOM RIGHT: *Nevada* at sea with other battleships in the 1920s.

Nevada class

The Nevadas were the first US battleships to carry a super-firing twin turret over a triple turret, thus contracting the heavy broadside into just four mountings. At the time they were also the most heavily armoured USN battleships, with the upper and lower belts merged into one with a maximum thickness of 340mm/13.5in. They were the first to use oil as their primary fuel and the last to have two shafts. *Nevada* had turbines and Yarrow boilers, while *Oklahoma* was the last USN battleship to have reciprocating steam engines (with Babcock and Wilcox boilers) which gave her a range of 12,875km/8,000 miles. They were originally completed with a large battery of anti-torpedo-boat 125mm/5in guns, but these were very exposed to the sea and were suppressed.

The Nevadas were based in Ireland in World War I, covering troop convoys to Europe. They were modernized in 1927–9, when gun elevation was increased, and two distinctive tripod masts were fitted as well as aircraft catapults. Anti-torpedo bulges increased the beam to 32.3m/106ft and additional anti-aircraft guns were added.

Both ships were sunk in the Japanese attack on Pearl Harbor on December 7, 1941. *Nevada* was the only battleship to get underway and became the main objective of the second wave of Japanese aircraft and was stranded. *Nevada* supported the landings at Attu in May 1943, Normandy and Southern France in 1944, and Iwo Jima and Okinawa in 1945, when she was hit by a suicide plane on March 27 and by shore artillery on April 5. Irradiated at Bikini in 1946, she was sunk off Hawaii.

In 1936 *Oklahoma* evacuated during the Spanish Civil War. At Pearl Harbor she was berthed outboard of the battleship *Maryland* and hit by a large number of aerial torpedoes. She rolled over and sank. Her salvage became a matter of pride but with a gaping hole in her side she was beyond repair. The hulk sank while under tow in 1947.

Nevada class

Class: *Nevada, Oklahoma.* Launched 1914
Dimensions: Length – 175.3m/575ft
   Beam – 29m/95ft
   Draught – 8.7m/28ft 6in
Displacement: 27,940 tonnes/27,500 tons
Armament: Main – 10 x 355mm/14in guns
Secondary – 21 x 125mm/5in guns and
   2 x 535mm/21in torpedoes
Machinery: 12 boilers, 2 shafts,
   20,880kW/26,000shp (*Nevada*)
   19,700kW/24,800shp (*Oklahoma*)
Speed: 20 knots
Complement: 864 men

LEFT: *Pennsylvania* at sea in May 1934, after her first modernization. One of the most significant features was the replacement of the cage masts by tripods, carrying considerably more fire control equipment than these ships used to have.

Pennsylvania class

Class: *Pennsylvania, Arizona.* Launched 1915
Dimensions: Length – 185.3m/608ft
Beam – 29.6m/97ft
Draught – 8.8m/29ft
Displacement: 31,900 tonnes/31,400 tons
Armament: Main – 12 x 355mm/14in guns
Secondary – 22 x 125mm/5in, 4 x 75mm/3in guns and 2 x 535mm/21in torpedoes
Machinery: 12 boilers, 4 shafts, 23,490kW/31,500shp
Speed: 21 knots
Complement: 915 men

Pennsylvania class

The Pennsylvanias were enlarged Nevadas, with four triple turrets. Reconstructed in 1929–31, they received the usual range of improvements. In addition *Pennsylvania*, designated as a flagship, was given a two-tier armoured conning tower. Both were in battleship row when the Japanese attacked Pearl Harbor. *Arizona* blew up and her remains are now an American national memorial.

Pennsylvania was in dry dock and only slightly damaged. Fitted with a large battery of anti-aircraft guns in late 1942, she supported many amphibious operations and was at the Battle of Surigao Strait on October 25, 1944.

On August 12, 1945, *Pennsylvania* was the last major warship to be hit during World War II. A target ship at atomic bomb tests in 1946, *Pennsylvania* was scuttled in 1948.

New Mexico class

LEFT: **An aerial view of *New Mexico* taken in 1919. Compare this photograph of *New Mexico,* more or less as newly completed with distinctive cage masts, and *Pennsylvania* after modernization. All these ships underwent further modernizations after Pearl Harbor in order to combat the threat from the air.**

Mississippi was converted to a gunnery training and weapons development ship in 1946, and in the 1950s to a test ship for the USN's first surface-to-air guided missile, Terrier. She was sold for scrap in 1956. *New Mexico* was hit twice by kamikaze planes, but was present in Tokyo Bay when Japan surrendered on September 2, 1945. She was sold for scrap in October 1947. *Idaho* was also present in Tokyo Bay and she was scrapped in November 1947.

New Mexico class

Class: *New Mexico, Mississippi, Idaho.*
Launched 1917
Dimensions: Length – 190m/624ft
Beam – 29.7m/97ft 5in
Draught – 9.1m/30ft
Displacement: 32,510 tonnes/32,000 tons
Armament: Main – 12 x 355mm/14in guns
Secondary – 14 x 125mm/5in, 4 x 75mm/3in guns and 2 x 535mm/21in torpedoes
Machinery: 9 boilers, 4 shafts, 23,862kW/32,000shp
Speed: 21 knots
Complement: 1,084 men

The New Mexico class had three triple turrets of an improved design. Some secondary armament was placed in the bow and stern, but had to be removed because they were too wet, and the remaining 125mm/5in guns were in the superstructure. A clipper bow made for better sea-keeping. Initially two ships were intended, but selling two pre-Dreadnoughts to Greece paid for a third. *New Mexico* had a new propulsion system, which had been trialled in the collier *Jupiter*. This used steam turbines to turn electrical generators, which in turn powered the ship's propellers driven by electric motors. All were rebuilt in 1931–4, receiving new superstructures, modern gun directors, new engines, deck armour and anti-torpedo bulges. All three were in the Atlantic in 1941 and so avoided the attack on Pearl Harbor, but were recalled and participated in many landing operations, and *Mississippi* took part in the Battle of Surigao Strait.

Kashima class

These two ships were the last pre-Dreadnoughts built in Britain for the Imperial Japanese Navy, and with one exception represented the last major Japanese warships built anywhere abroad. They were the equivalent of the King Edward VII class. No doubt

Japanese officers standing by their ships in Britain would have had plenty of time to study developments in battleship design. The Imperial Japanese Navy had already drawn up plans for an 18,290-tonne/18,000-ton cruiser with 255mm/10in guns, and the lessons of the

Russo-Japanese War confirmed to the Japanese their subsequent choice of an all-big-gun ship. *Kashima* and *Katori* saw no action and were broken up in 1924.

LEFT: *Kashima* was the last pre-Dreadnought built for the Imperial Japanese Navy, with 305mm/12in and 255mm/10in guns.

Kashima class

Class: *Kashima, Katori.* Launched 1905
Dimensions: Length – 144.3m/473ft 7in
  Beam – 23.8m/78ft 2in
  Draught – 8m/26ft 4in
Displacement: 16,663 tonnes/16,400 tons
Armament: Main – 4 x 305mm/12in and
  4 x 255mm/10in guns
  Secondary – 12 x 50mm/2in guns and
  5 x 455mm/18in torpedoes
Machinery: 20 boilers, 2 shafts,
  11,782kW/15,800shp
Speed: 18.5 knots
Complement: 946 men

Satsuma class

The Satsuma class is further proof that the idea of an all-big-gun ship arose in several places at about the same time. These ships had been designed before the Battle of Tsushima and were to be armed with 12 305mm/12in guns. However, impoverished by the Russo-Japanese War, the Imperial Japanese Navy could not afford both the 305mm/12in guns it wanted to buy from Britain and the Curtis turbines from the USA. Hence these ships were completed with a mixed armament, all in turrets.

The Japanese learned quickly, and *Aki* benefited from the lessons learned in building *Satsuma*, and the 120mm/4.7in guns were replaced by 150mm/6in guns as the secondary armament. The Japanese did not have the same problems as the USN in making turbines work in their ships and they quickly abandoned the reciprocating steam engine, though a shortage of oil meant that the Japanese used coal-fired boilers for longer than most navies. There were minor differences in size between these

LEFT: *Satsuma,* seen here before her launch, and *Aki* were to be all-big-gun ships but the Japanese ran out of cash to buy all the guns they required.

two half-sisters, and *Aki* had three instead of two funnels. Both ships were disarmed under the terms of the Washington Naval Treaty. They were unsuitable for modernization, and expended as targets in 1924.

Satsuma class

Class: *Satsuma, Aki.* Launched 1906–7
Dimensions: Length – 146.9m/482ft
  Beam – 25.5m/83ft 6in
  Draught – 8.4m/27ft 6in
Displacement: 19,683 tonnes/19,372 tons
Armament: Main – 4 x 305mm/12in and
  12 x 255mm/10in guns
  Secondary – 12 x 120mm/4.7in guns and
  5 x 455mm/18in torpedoes
Machinery: 20 boilers, 2 shafts,
  12,901kW/17,300ihp
Speed: 18.25 knots
Complement: 887 men

Tsukuba class

The Imperial Japanese Navy had a preference for speed and armament over armour, and this included both large battlecruisers and small ones like *Tsukuba* and *Ikoma*. Built as armoured cruisers (when the Royal Navy introduced the term) these were re-rated as battlecruisers and were ordered to replace earlier pre-Dreadnought battleships. Japanese industry, including shipbuilding, was advancing rapidly and

with these and successor ships they demonstrated their ability to build quickly. Nevertheless, despite their rapid construction, by the time these ships were completed in 1907–8 other navies were building yet bigger and faster battlecruisers. *Tsukuba* was a defect-prone ship and suffered an ammunition explosion in 1917. *Ikoma* was re-armed in 1919 as a training ship before being scrapped in 1924.

Tsukuba class	

Class: *Tsukuba, Ikoma*. Launched 1905–6
Dimensions: Length – 137.2m/450ft
  Beam – 23m/75ft 5in
  Draught – 7.9m/26ft 1in
Displacement: 13,970 tonnes/13,750 tons
Armament: Main – 4 x 305mm/12in and
  12 x 150mm/6in guns
  Secondary – 12 x 120mm/4.7in guns and
  3 x 455mm/18in torpedoes
Machinery: 20 boilers, 2 shafts,
  15,287kW/20,500ihp
Speed: 20.5 knots
Complement: 879 men

Ibuki class

Ibuki class	

Class: *Ibuki, Kurama*. Launched 1907
Dimensions: Length – 147.8m/485ft
  Beam – 23m/75ft 4in
  Draught – 7.9m/26ft 1in
Displacement: 14,870 tonnes/14,636 tons
Armament: Main – 4 x 305mm/12in and
  8 x 205mm/8in guns
  Secondary – 14 x 120mm/4.7in guns and
  3 x 455mm/18in torpedoes
Machinery: 20 boilers, 2 shafts,
  16,778kW/22,500ihp
Speed: 20.5 knots
Complement: 844 men

The Ibuki class was an improved Tsukuba class. *Ibuki* was delayed because the slips at Kure were occupied and she was re-engineered with turbines. Few Japanese ships saw any action in World War I, but *Ibuki* joined the hunt in

the Pacific for the German East Asiatic Squadron. She also escorted convoys of Australian and New Zealand troops across the Indian Ocean in 1914. Warships also operated in support of the Allies in the eastern Mediteranean.

LEFT: *Fuso* in dry dock at Kure. *Fuso* and *Yamashiro* when completed were powerful, elegant ships, but were rebuilt with thick control towers and single funnels in the 1930s. Unlike the Kashima, Satsuma, Tsukuba and Ibuki classes, which were all too small, the 30,480-tonne/30,600-ton *Fuso* and *Yamashiro* incorporated all the lessons of the Dreadnought revolution and were capable of a worthwhile and significant mid-life update which enabled them to see action in World War II.
BELOW: *Yamashiro* at sea in 1934.

Fuso class

The Fuso class was the first of super-Dreadnoughts with guns greater than 305mm/12in. Reckoned by some to be too lightly armoured for their size, the Japanese applied the lesson they had learned from mine and torpedo damage during the Russo-Japanese War and fitted their ships with much greater subdivision of compartments in order to control this damage.

After World War I both ships acquired additional searchlights and improved gun-direction platforms, and *Yamashiro* received a British-style flying-off ramp on B turret. Both ships were extensively modernized in the 1930s. They were lengthened by some 7.6m/25ft, and their beam increased by over 3.7m/12ft with anti-torpedo bulges. New turbines and space-saving boilers nearly doubled their horsepower from 29,828kW/40,000shp to 55,928kW/75,000shp and increased speed by nearly 2 knots, despite the weight of additional deck armour. The change from coal- to oil-fired boilers also increased the ships' range.

Both ships were equipped with aircraft and a catapult, which was mounted on the quarterdeck in *Yamashiro* and initially

over Q turret in *Fuso* until removed to the quarterdeck. The secondary and anti-aircraft armament was improved and the elevation of the main guns increased to 43 degrees, giving the 355mm/14in guns a range of 22km/13.5 miles. In the conversion, the fore funnel was done away with entirely, and the elegant tripod mast of the original design was replaced by towering pagodas containing conning positions, light guns, searchlights, rangefinders and gun direction platforms.

Fuso and *Yamashiro* operated together during World War II, either as the covering force to long-range convoys or awaiting the decisive battle which the Japanese thought the Americans might attempt, as the Russians had 40 years before. They were also sunk together.

At the Battle of Surigao Strait on October 25, 1944, *Fuso* and *Yamashiro* encountered a USN fleet which included the six battleships *Mississippi, Maryland, West Virginia, Tennessee, California* and *Pennsylvania*. *Fuso* was sunk by gunfire and *Yamashiro* succumbed to a massed torpedo attack by USN destroyers – although experts are still arguing as to which ship was sunk first and, in the darkness, how.

Fuso class	

Class: *Fuso, Yamashiro*. Launched 1914–15
Dimensions: Length – 203m/665ft
   Beam – 28.6m/94ft
   Draught – 8.7m/28ft 6in
Displacement: 30,480 tonnes/30,600 tons
Armament: Main – 12 x 355mm/14in guns
   Secondary – 16 x 150mm/6in,
   4 x 80mm/3.1in guns and 6 x 535mm/21in torpedoes
Machinery: 24 boilers, 4 shafts,
   29,828kW/40,000shp
Speed: 22.5 knots
Complement: 1,193 men

Kongo class

The battlecruiser *Kongo* was the very last Japanese capital ship to be built outside Japan. While *Kongo* was designed and built by Vickers, large components were delivered from Britain to Japan for *Kongo*'s three sister ships. *Kongo* was intended as a model ship for Japanese shipyards to emulate, but her evident success, and superiority over the British Lion class which was building at the same time, inspired the changes which led to the Tiger class.

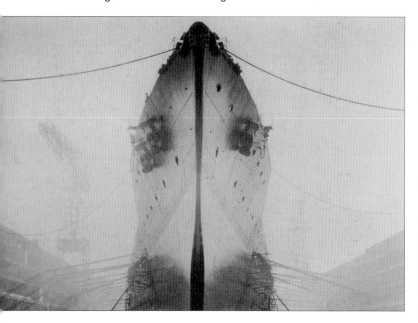

After World War I all four ships were refitted and received pagoda-like control towers, and funnel cowls, and were re-designated as battleships. They were modernized in 1936–7 when the hull was lengthened, and with new machinery they could reach over 30 knots. High speed and heavy guns made the Kongo class useful ships which saw much action in World War II. The Japanese concept was that the Kongos should act as escorts to carrier battle groups. Modifications during World War II to *Kongo* and *Haruna* included the fitting of radar. All ships of the class were sunk in the war.

In December 1941, *Kongo* supported the Japanese invasion of the Malayan Peninsula. She then supported landings in Java, and was part of the force which raided the Indian Ocean. At the Battle of Midway in June 1942, *Kongo* was part of the covering force, and during the Guadalcanal campaign she bombarded Henderson airfield, took part in the Battle of the Santa Cruz Islands and the naval Battle of Guadalcanal. Then in June 1944 she performed her intended function as part of the Japanese carrier escort force at the Battle of the Philippine

TOP: **The battleship *Kongo* from a postcard in the 1920s. Japanese sailors were proud of their ships and wanted postcards to send home. *Kongo* was the last major unit built abroad for the Imperial Japanese Navy, primarily for Japanese constructors to gain experience of the latest British methods. The three other ships of the same class were Japanese-built.** LEFT: **A rare picture of *Kongo* in dry dock at Yokosuka during her reconstruction during the 1930s.**

LEFT: **Four Japanese battleships photographed pre-war:** *Nagato, Kirishima, Ise* **and** *Hyuga*. **The Japanese fleet was powerful but, as the profiles of these ships show, photographed in the 1930s, it relied on a core of World War I ships which had been modernized and some inter-war ships which had not been built in large batches nor followed the same generational and incremental steps from which American and British battleships had benefited.** BELOW: *Haruna* **was sunk at Edashima in April 1945 by USN carrier aircraft.**

Sea. At the Battle of Leyte Gulf, *Kongo* showed her immense strength, surviving a torpedoing, naval air attacks, and a bombing from high level. However, on November 21, 1944, she was torpedoed by the USN submarine *Sealion*, causing a fire which raged out of control until she blew up and sank. *Kongo* was the only battleship to be sunk by a submarine attack during the war in the Pacific.

Like her sisters, *Kirishima* was modernized in 1927–30, rebuilt in 1935–6, and reclassified as a battleship. She was part of the escort force during the Japanese attack on Pearl Harbor and in spring 1942 part of the fleet that raided the Indian Ocean. Active throughout that year, she received minor damage during a skirmish on November 13. Off Savo Island two nights later she was disabled by the USN battleship *Washington*, during the last ever purely battleship-to-battleship engagement, and was scuttled by her crew.

Haruna was damaged by a mine laid by the German auxiliary cruiser *Wolf* in 1917. In December 1941 she covered the landings in Malaya and in early 1942 she supported the Japanese conquest of the Dutch East Indies. *Haruna* was present at most significant battles throughout 1942: in June she was damaged at the Battle of Midway and in October (with *Kongo*) she devastated Henderson airfield. With the bulk of the Japanese fleet, *Haruna* was held back in Japan for a decisive battle against the US Navy during 1943–4. She was hit by a bomb in June 1944 at the Battle of the Philippine Sea, and also survived the Battle of Leyte Gulf. Damaged by near-misses in October 1944, *Haruna* was finally sunk at Kure by carrier aircraft on July 28, 1945.

Hiei was the only one of her class to be demilitarized under the terms of the Washington Naval Treaty. However, in the 1930s she received the same modernization as her sisters and returned to the Japanese order of battle. She was present at the attack on Pearl Harbor, the invasion of the Dutch East Indies, and the Japanese sortie into the Indian Ocean. During

the campaign off Guadalcanal she showed great resilience, like *Kirishima*, surviving more than 100 hits from the USN cruisers *Portland* and *San Francisco*, and torpedoes from the destroyers *Cushing* and *O'Bannon*. She was finally hit and sunk by high-level bombing on November 13, 1942.

Kongo class

Class: *Kongo, Hiei, Haruna, Kirishima.*
  Launched 1912–13
Dimensions: Length – 215m/704ft
  Beam– 28m/92ft
  Draught – 8.5m/27ft 7in
Displacement: 27,940 tonnes/27,500 tons
Armament: Main – 8 x 355mm/14in guns
  Secondary – 16 x 150mm/6in,
  8 x 80mm/3.1in guns and
  8 x 535mm/21in torpedoes
Machinery: 36 boilers, 4 shafts,
  47,725kW/64,000shp
Speed: 27.5 knots
Complement: 1,221 men

Ise class

These were improved versions of the Fuso class, being slightly longer and larger. The midships P turret was moved and raised into a super-firing position over Q turret, thus making better use of the between decks and enabling an improved machinery room space.

They were modernized in two stages. In 1926–8 the two tripod masts were replaced by a pole mainmast and a pagoda foremast, the fore funnel received a cowl, and a catapult was mounted on X turret (this was removed to the quarterdeck in 1933). Total conversion followed in the 1930s, when they were lengthened, the armour increased, bulges fitted, boilers upgraded, fore funnel suppressed, main gun elevation improved and they received additional light guns.

After the Battle of Midway, both ships were modified into semi-aircraft carriers. The after turrets were suppressed and a short flight deck installed, with two

TOP: *Ise* was launched in 1916 and with her sisters modernized in the 1920s. ABOVE: *Hyuga* sitting on the bottom at Kure after an air attack in 1945. RIGHT: A close-up of B turret. The forward turret is submerged.

powerful catapults, however neither ship seems to have carried aircraft and the concept was never proved.

Hyuga was at the Battle of Midway, and converted to a semi-carrier in 1942–3. However, she saw action as a battleship during the battle for Leyte Gulf. She received some damage and was sent to Kure for repairs, where she was bombed again in March and July 1945. She settled on the bottom on July 24, where she was broken up in 1946.

Ise followed an almost identical career, and was sunk on July 27, 1945.

Ise class

Class: *Ise, Hyuga.* Launched 1916–17
Dimensions: Length – 206m/675ft
  Beam – 28.6m/94ft
  Draught – 8.9m/29ft 1in
Displacement: 31,762 tonnes/31,260 tons
Armament: Main – 12 x 355mm/14in guns
  Secondary – 20 x 140mm/5.5in,
  4 x 80mm/3.1in guns and
  6 x 535mm/21in torpedoes
Machinery: 24 boilers, 4 shafts,
  33,557kW/45,000shp
Speed: 22.5 knots
Complement: 1,360 men

Nassau class

A battleship considerably more powerful than the archetypal pre-Dreadnought was being contemplated by the German navy when the news of Fisher's *Dreadnought* spread abroad. The consequence was a three-year delay while the Germans worked out exactly what Fisher had achieved. The resulting design was the first German Dreadnought, with 12 large-calibre guns in a hexagonal layout of twin turrets. This was not ideal as only a maximum of four turrets could be brought to bear on any one target, but the Germans rationalized that the two turrets on the disengaged side formed a reserve. These ships were easily identified by the two prominent gooseneck cranes carried amidships. The Nassau class rolled dangerously even on a smooth sea and bilge keels had to be fitted.

The class operated as a unit and in April 1916 were part of the covering force during the German bombardment of Scarborough and Yarmouth. At the Battle of Jutland, *Nassau* was hit twice and soon repaired, *Westfalen* and *Rheinland* were both hit once and slightly damaged, and *Posen* was undamaged.

In August and again in October 1916 attempted sorties into the North Sea were frustrated, but in April 1918 *Nassau* progressed as far as the latitude of Stavanger, Norway, before turning back without achieving very much. *Westfalen* was torpedoed by the British submarine *E-23* in August 1916 but repaired.

In 1918 *Westfalen* was sent into the Baltic to assist the Finns in their uprising against the Russians and the ensuing civil war. *Rheinland* accompanied *Westfalen* to the Baltic, but ran aground in April 1918 off the Åland islands. She was salvaged (involving the removal of 6,503 tonnes/6,400 tons of coal, armour, ammunition and guns) three months later and was towed to Kiel where she became a barracks ship.

Posen first entered the Baltic and then accompanied *Nassau* north to Norway. All ships of the class were deleted from the German navy in November 1919. *Nassau* was allocated to Japan, and *Westfalen* and *Posen* were allocated to Britain. All ships of the class were scrapped in 1920–4 under the terms of the Armistice, leaving Germany with only some very obsolete battleships.

Nassau class

Class: *Nassau, Westfalen, Rheinland, Posen.* Launched 1908
Dimensions: Length – 137.7m/451ft 9in
Beam – 26.9m/88ft 5in
Draught – 8.1m/26ft 6in
Displacement: 18,870 tonnes/18,570 tons
Armament: Main – 12 x 280mm/11in guns
Secondary – 12 x 150mm/6in,
16 x 88mm/3.46in guns and
6 x 455mm/18in torpedoes
Machinery: 12 boilers, 3 shafts,
16,405kW/22,000ihp
Speed: 19.5 knots
Complement: 1,008 men

BELOW: **A starboard bow view of the *panzerkreuzer Westfalen*.** BOTTOM: **The four ships of the Nassau class, *Nassau*, *Westfalen*, *Rheinland* and *Posen*, alongside, possibly in pre-war Hamburg.**

ABOVE LEFT: **The German battle fleet at sea.** *Oldenburg* **is nearest to the camera.** ABOVE: **Post-war** *Ostfriesland* **was sunk during aerial bombing trials by the USAAF.** LEFT: **The bombing trials were somewhat artificial as the targets were both stationary and not firing back at the bombers. Nevertheless, although it took several attempts by the bombers to get photographic evidence like this, the pictures had a powerful influence on decision-makers in the USA.**

Helgoland class

While retaining the inefficient hexagon layout of the main armament, the Helgolands were a considerable improvement over their predecessors. Compared with the Dreadnoughts building in Britain, they were like most German ships of this period, lighter and beamier. They also had better internal subdivision and greater pumping power, and the German ammunition was safer when hit because it was inclined to burn rather than explode. The Germans retained reciprocating steam engines for longer than the Royal Navy, but this class introduced the 305mm/12in gun to the German navy.

The class acted as a unit, and was part of the covering force for the bombardment of Scarborough and Yarmouth in April 1916, and fought at Jutland in May. *Helgoland* and *Oldenburg* received one hit each and were quickly repaired. *Ostfriesland* hit a mine but was repaired by the end of July. All ships took

part in the Battle of Dogger Bank, but were inactive for most of the remainder of the war. After Germany's defeat in World War I, *Helgoland, Ostfriesland, Thüringen* and *Oldenburg* were handed over to Britain, USA, France and Japan respectively.

Interned at Scapa Flow, *Ostfriesland* was not scuttled with the rest of the German High Seas Fleet because she had been moved to Rosyth, prior to being taken over by the USN. She was steamed to New York where she was decommissioned and dry-docked so that USN naval architects could examine her design. She was then expended as a target in July 1921 while at anchor. *Ostfriesland* survived many bomb hits and near-misses. She would probably have avoided any damage if she had been underway and, even if hit, been saved if damage control measures had been taken. Carefully edited film of her eventual sinking was used to help

promote the use of air power. In 1920 *Thüringen* survived an attempted scuttling off Cherbourg by her German crew. In 1920s she was used as a target, then was sold for scrap. A large portion of the hull still remains off the beach at Gavres and continued to be used for target practice until the 1990s.

Helgoland class

Class: *Helgoland, Ostfriesland,Thüringen, Oldenburg.* Launched 1909–10
Dimensions: Length – 167.2m/548ft 7in
   Beam – 28.5m/93ft 6in
   Draught – 8.2m/26ft 11in
Displacement: 22,800 tonnes/22,440 tons
Armament: Main – 12 x 305mm/12in guns
   Secondary – 14 x 150mm/6in,
   14 x 88mm/3.46in guns and
   6 x 510mm/20in torpedoes
Machinery: 15 boilers, 3 shafts,
   20,880kW/28,000ihp
Speed: 20 knots
Complement: 1,113 men

LEFT: *Prinzregent Luitpold* immediately pre-war showing off the range and elevation of her 305mm/12in guns.

Kaiser class

The Kaisers were the first German battleships to be fitted with turbines and with an oil-burning capability. Like other German ships they had three (rather than the British arrangement of four) propellers. It was intended to provide *Prinzregent Luitpold* with a diesel to drive her central shaft but this was not fitted and the space was left empty. The use of turbines made it easier to mount the midships guns *en echelon*, and with one after turret mounted in a super-firing position the Kaisers – despite having one less turret compared with their predecessors – could still bring one more turret (all five) to bear on either beam.

Kaiser took part in most of the German naval operations of World War I in the North Sea: the bombardments of the English east cost, the First and Second Battles of Heligoland Bight, the Battle of Dogger Bank and the Battle of Jutland, where she was hit twice. In 1917 she also operated in the Baltic. All four sister ships followed similar careers. In addition, *Friedrich der Grosse* was flagship of the German High Seas fleet until March 1917.

Kaiser class

Class: *Kaiser, Friedrich der Grosse, Kaiserin, König Albert, Prinzregent Luitpold.* Launched 1911–12.
Dimensions: Length – 172m/564ft
Beam – 29m/95ft 3in
Draught – 8.3m/27ft 3in
Displacement: 25,095 tonnes/24,700 tons
Armament: Main – 10 x 305m/12in guns
Secondary – 14 x 150mm/6in guns and 5 x 510mm/20in torpedoes
Machinery: 18 boilers, 3 shafts, 18,640kW/25,000hp
Speed: 21 knots
Complement: 1,088 men

König class

LEFT: The *linienschiff König* from a pre-war postcard. The class was new at the time of Jutland, where they saw much fighting, and they also fought in the Baltic.

These ships followed the pattern of operations for the High Sea Fleet and were in the thick of the fighting at Jutland, firing between them some 700 rounds of 305mm/12in munitions. They received hits as follows: *König*, ten; *Grosser Kurfürst,* eight; *Markgraf,* five. *Kronprinz* escaped undamaged. *König* went on to destroy the Russian battleship *Slava* on October 17, 1917, in the Baltic. Commander Noel Laurence in the British submarine *J-1* has the distinction of being the only submariner to hit two battleships in one go, when he fired a salvo of torpedoes at *Kronprinz* and *Grosser Kurfürst* on November 5, 1916, but in neither case was the damage fatal. *Kronprinz* was renamed *Kronprinz Wilhelm* in 1918.

Grosser Kurfürst holds something of a record for accidents: she collided with *König* in December 1914, ran aground in 1917, collided with *Kronprinz* also in 1917, hit a mine in the same year, damaged herself entering Wilhelmshaven in 1918, and ran aground off Heligoland on May 30, 1918.

All ships of both the Kaiser and König classes were interned at Scapa Flow and scuttled on June 21, 1921. They were then broken up from the 1930s onwards.

König class

Class: *König, Grosser Kurfürst, Markgraf, Kronprinz (Wilhelm).* Launched 1913
Dimensions: Length – 177m/580ft
Beam – 29m/96ft
Draught – 8.4m/27ft 6in
Displacement: 25,910 tonnes/25,000 tons
Armament: Main – 10 x 305mm/12in guns
Secondary – 14 x 150mm/6in guns and 5 x 510mm/20in torpedoes
Machinery: 18 boilers, 3 shafts, 25,350kW/34,000hp
Speed: 21.5 knots
Complement: 1,100 men

Bayern class

LEFT: *Baden* seen here pre-war as fleet flagship. Neither ship was available in time for *Der Tag* (the Battle of Jutland) and they were the last Dreadnought battleships to be completed for the German Kaiser's navy. Others were planned and even laid down, but all were cancelled. ABOVE: *Bayern* had a relatively short life. She was laid down in 1914, launched in 1915 and scuttled in 1919. BELOW LEFT: *Bayern*, showing the German three-shaft arrangement, being towed to the breakers in 1935. BELOW: *Bayern* was mined in the Gulf of Riga in 1917.

This class introduced the 380mm/15in gun to the German navy as well as double-ended super-firing turrets, which meant that with just four twin turrets, all guns could fire over wide arcs on the beam. The German navy considered fitting triple turrets, but after studying the Austro-Hungarian battleships of the Viribus Unitis class, they decided against it on the grounds of weight, ammunition supply, rate of fire, torque and loss of fighting capability should one turret be hit. Instead the Germans opted for the larger-calibre gun. The two outer shafts were turbine-driven, and the centre line shaft was diesel-driven.

Bayern and Baden missed the Battle of Jutland but Bayern supported German landings in the Gulf of Riga in October 1917 against Russian-held positions. Ten German battleships were opposed by two Russian pre-Dreadnoughts, cruisers and three small British C-class submarines. Off Moon (Muhu) in the northern entrance to the gulf Bayern and Grosser Kurfürst hit mines on October 12, and Bayern suffered serious flooding through her forward underwater torpedo flat.

However, on October 17, the battleships König and Kronprinz damaged the Russian pre-Dreadnought Slava so badly that she had to be scuttled, and hit Grazdanin (formerly Tsessarevitch) which retired to the east and north. The badly flooded Bayern did not reach Kiel until October 31. She was scuttled at Scapa Flow and broken up in 1934–5. Baden took over from Friedrich der Grosse as flagship of the German High Fleet. She saw no action and was scuttled at Scapa Flow but beached by the British before she could sink, and eventually expended as a target during battleship practice in 1921.

Two slightly larger ships, Sachsen and Württemberg, were laid down in 1913 and 1914 but not completed and broken up on the slips in 1921.

Another class of fast battleship, this time with 420mm/16.5in guns, was designed but work on these ships was never started.

Bayern class

Class: *Bayern, Baden.*
  Launched 1913-15
Dimensions: Length – 179.8m/589ft 10in
  Beam – 30m/98ft 5in
  Draught – 8.4m/27ft 8in
Displacement: 28,525 tonnes/28,074 tons
Armament: Main – 8 x 380mm/15in guns
  Secondary – 16 x 150mm/6in,
  8 x 88mm/3.46in guns and
  5 x 600mm/23.6in torpedoes
Machinery: 14 boilers, 3 shafts.
  35,794kW/48,000shp
Speed: 21 knots
Complement: 1,187 men

Von der Tann

Starting in 1908 the Hamburg shipyard of Blohm and Voss built a series of successful battlecruisers, the first ship in response to the British Invincible class being *Von der Tann*.

This first German battlecruiser was bigger all-round than the *Invincible*, and more heavily armoured. Anti-roll tanks were originally fitted but these proved ineffective and bilge keels were installed instead and the additional space was used for extra fuel. *Von der Tann* was also the first German capital ship to have turbines. Although the speed was about the same, her endurance was greater. The secondary armament (150mm/6in) was heavier than the *Invincible*'s (100mm/4in), and the German 280mm/11in main gun was almost as good as the British 305mm/12in, while the British ammunition was inferior. Although the midships turrets were placed *en echelon*, they were far enough inboard to have a good arc of fire on the opposite beam, and in most situations the broadside consisted of eight guns as compared to *Invincible*'s six. German ships generally had more thorough damage control arrangements, and so *Von der Tann* was a much better design and a superior warship to the Invincibles.

Von der Tann was present at most of the major naval engagements of World War I, starting with the Battle of Heligoland Bight in August 1914. She bombarded the English towns of Yarmouth on November 3, 1914, Scarborough on December 16, 1914, and Lowestoft on April 24, 1915.

At Jutland *Von der Tann* engaged *Indefatigable,* where one salvo caused an explosion in X magazine and another hit *Indefatigable*'s forecastle, whereupon she blew up, after only a quarter of an hour of the first phase of the battle. By comparison *Von der Tann* was also hit but withstood the damage. Two 380mm/15in and two 340mm/13.5in rounds put two turrets out of action and damaged two others, and she was without her main armament for one hour and fifteen minutes, but she was fully repaired by August 1916.

Her other sorties were less successful and late in 1916 and again in 1917 she required repairs to her turbines. She was scuttled with the rest of the German High Seas Fleet, but raised in 1903 and broken up at Rosyth in 1931–4.

BELOW: *Von der Tann* photographed in 1910 before she was handed over to the German navy. She was reckoned to be a considerably better fighting ship than any British battlecruiser, primarily because she could withstand more damage. RIGHT: *Von der Tann* under tow to the breakers. Some of the work was contracted abroad and these tugs, in the mid 1930s, are flying the Nazi swastika.

Von der Tann

Class: *Von der Tann.* Launched 1909
Dimensions: Length – 171.7m/563ft 4in
  Beam – 26.6m/87ft 3in
  Draught – 8.1m/26ft 6in
Displacement: 19,370 tonnes/19,064 tons
Armament: Main – 8 x 280mm/11in guns
  Secondary – 10 x 150mm/6in,
  16 x 88mm/3.46in guns and
  4 x 455mm/18in torpedoes
Machinery: 18 boilers, 4 shafts.
  32,513kw/43,600shp
Speed: 24.75 knots
Complement: 923 men

Moltke and *Goeben*

*M*oltke and *Goeben* were further improvements over *Von der Tann*, being slightly larger, with a streamlined hull form and, as with *Von der Tann*, bilge keels replaced the anti-rolling tanks. The main improvement and external difference was an additional super-firing after turret, bringing the broadside up to a possible ten 280mm/11in guns.

Moltke was present at most surface actions in World War I, took part in the bombardment of the English east coast and was torpedoed twice. She was hit forward by a torpedo fired by Lieutenant Commander Noel Lawrence of *E-1* (who would later torpedo *Kronprinz* and *Grosser Kürfurst* while in command of the submarine *J-1*) on August 19, 1915, in the Gulf of Riga but the damage was slight. On April 25, 1918, during a sortie by the German High Seas Fleet, *Moltke* lost a propeller, damaged the water inlet of one of her condensers and an engine room was flooded. She was under tow by *Oldenburg* when she was torpedoed by *E-42*; nevertheless she reached Germany and was repaired. Scuttled at

Scapa Flow, *Moltke* was raised in 1927 and broken up in 1927–9.

Goeben was flagship of the German Mediterranean division and was visiting Trieste when World War I broke out. Under the command of Admiral Souchon she made a feint against French troop convoys assembling in North Africa and then made a dash for the Bosphorus, chased unsuccessfully by the British *Indomitable* and *Indefatigable*. Once she arrived at Constantinople she was sold to Turkey, to replace capital ships which the British had confiscated, and played a major role in turning the balance of power in the region. The renamed *Yavuz* saw active service in the Black Sea, including some of the few engagements between pre-Dreadnoughts and Dreadnoughts, and she sank the British monitors *Raglan* and *M-28* on January 20, 1918, but ran into a minefield. She survived until 1974.

TOP: **The battlecruiser *Moltke*, photographed pre-war.** ABOVE: ***Moltke* being towed under the Forth Bridge on her way to the breakers at Rosyth.**

Moltke class

Class: *Moltke, Goeben.* Launched 1910

Dimensions: Length – 186.5m/611ft 11in
Beam – 29.5m/96ft 10in
Draught – 9m/29ft 5in

Displacement: 22,979 tonnes/22,616 tons

Armament: Main – 10 x 280mm/11in guns
Secondary – 12 x 150mm/6in,
12 x 88mm/3.46in guns and
4 x 510mm/20in torpedoes

Machinery: 24 boilers, 4 shafts,
38,776kW/52,000shp

Speed: 25.5 knots

Complement: 1,053 men

LEFT: **The damaged *Seydlitz*, down by the bows, after the Battle of Jutland. Despite the damage she was able to return to Germany for repair, before eventually being scuttled at Scarpa Flow and raised for scrap in 1928.**

Seydlitz

Class: *Seydlitz*. Launched 1912
Dimensions: Length – 200.5m/657ft 11in
Beam – 28.5m/93ft 6in
Draught – 8.2m/26ft 11in
Displacement: 24,989 tonnes/24,594 tons
Armament: Main – 10 x 280mm/11in guns
Secondary – 12 x 150mm/6in,
12 x 88mm/3.46in guns and
4 x 510mm/20in torpedoes
Machinery: 27 boilers, 4 shafts,
46,979kW/63,000shp
Speed: 26.5 knots
Complement: 1,068 men

Seydlitz

Blohm and Voss continued their incremental changes to their battlecruisers. *Seydlitz* was larger again than the Moltke class and had a raised forecastle and the forward turret was one deck higher. Anti-rolling tanks still featured, but were not used. Like her predecessors *Seydlitz* had tandem rudders, but the forward rudder was ineffective and all these ships had excessively large turning circles. The British obtained the plans for *Seydlitz*

although they were not influenced by them. At the Battle of Dogger Bank *Seydlitz* received two or three 340mm/13.5in hits from *Lion* that caused a rapid fire that burned out both after turrets. During the raid on Lowestoft she struck a mine and shipped nearly 1,524 tonnes/1,500 tons of sea water.

At Jutland, *Seydlitz* fired on *Queen Mary* and helped to sink her. She also received a score of large-calibre hits herself and was torpedoed twice by the

destroyer *Petard* (or maybe *Turbulent*). Both after turrets were again burned out, and she shipped 5,385 tonnes/5,300 tons of water, increasing her draught to 14m/46ft. However, like other German designs which had good subdivision, *Seydlitz* proved capable of sustaining much damage. She reached Germany and was repaired at Wilhelmshaven. She was interned, scuttled at Scapa Flow and then raised for scrap in November 1928.

Derfflinger class

LEFT: ***Lützow*, one of the three Derfflinger class, was sunk at the Battle of Jutland in 1916. This proved to be the exception and other ships, such as *Seydlitz* above, proved to be very resistant to British firepower in battle.**

Hindenburg was completed too late for Jutland, saw little action and was scuttled at Scapa Flow. She was broken up in 1931–2.

Derfflinger class

Class: *Derfflinger, Lützow, Hindenburg.*
Launched 1913–15
Dimensions: Length – 210.4m/690ft 3in
Beam – 29m/95ft 2in
Draught – 8.3m/27ft 3in
Displacement: 26,600 tonnes/26,180 tons
Armament: Main – 8 x 305mm/12in guns
Secondary – 12 x 150mm/6in,
4 x 88m/3.46in guns and
4 torpedoes of various sizes
Machinery: 18 boilers, 4 shafts,
46,979kW/63,000shp
Speed: 26.5 knots
Complement: 1,112 men
Hindenburg's displacement was 26,938 tonnes/
26,513 tons. *Hindenburg* was 2.44m/8ft longer.
The secondary armament and size of torpedoes
varied across the class.

Flush-decked and with a pronounced sheer which became characteristic of later German warships, the Derfflingers had two super-firing turrets at each end. At the Battle of Dogger Bank *Derfflinger* was hit by three 340mm/13.5in shells, causing superficial damage. At Jutland she fired on *Queen Mary* and *Invincible,* which both blew up, but *Derfflinger* was hit by a score of heavy rounds, including ten 340mm/13.5in shells from *Revenge*. Both after turrets were put out of action,

fires started and she was flooded, but she was repaired by October 1916. She was interned, scuttled and raised at Scapa Flow in 1934 and her remains were finally scrapped in 1948.

At Jutland *Lützow* is credited with sinking *Invincible*, and probably the cruiser *Defence*, but took at least 24 heavy shells and was badly damaged. Her crew was rescued by a German torpedo boat who then torpedoed *Lützow*, which sank in two minutes.

Courbet class

The French navy was late in entering the Dreadnought race, and then built these four low-profile racy-looking ships, though following French procurement methods each was built at a different yard. Armed with twelve 305mm/12in guns, the forward and after guns were in super-firing turrets but the two wing turrets could only fire on their respective beams. Unlike the Dreadnought prototype, they also carried a substantial battery of medium-calibre guns. The thickness of the armour was generally less in these ships than in equivalent American and British battleships, but a minimum of 180mm/7in armour was carried well below the waterline. Originally they also carried a small outfit of mines: however, though some battleships were used as minelayers, it was not a happy combination of functions. The medium-calibre armament was suppressed in the 1920s and 1930s when these ships were also fitted with new boilers and the funnel arrangements were altered. In 1918 *Courbet* carried an observation balloon, and in 1920 *Paris* experimented with an aircraft ramp over B turret.

Jean Bart was completed in time to carry the French President on a pre-war state visit to St Petersburg in July 1914. In accordance with joint British and French naval plans, all four ships were employed in the Mediterranean during World War I, and on August 16, 1914, were involved in a battle off the Albanian coast in which the Austro-Hungarian cruiser *Zenta*

BELOW: **In 1940 some of the French fleet escaped to England. This close-up of** *Courbet* **shows British sailors cheering for the camera. After** *Courbet* **reverted to the Free French navy, she was grounded as an anti-aircraft battery off Ouistreham during the Normandy landings.**

LEFT: **Although they were a long time building and obsolescent when complete, the Courbet class (except for *France* which was wrecked in 1922) lasted until World War II.** BELOW: **The funnel arrangements and tall thin pole of military masts were reminiscent of some Italian designs of battleships. The layout lacks control equipment and rangefinders high over the ship, which nearly every other navy found essential for operations. These ships were not risked in the North Sea against the German High Sea Fleet.**

was sunk. *Jean Bart* was heavily damaged by the Austro-Hungarian submarine *U-12* in the Strait of Otranto in December 1914 and repaired at Malta. These modern ships were not risked during the Dardanelles campaign, but in 1919 *Jean Bart* took part in operations in the Black Sea against the Bolsheviks. *France* ran aground in Quiberon Bay in 1922 and was wrecked. *Jean Bart* (renamed *Ocean* in 1937) was scuttled in Toulon, used by the Germans as a target, and sunk by the Allies in 1944. *Paris* and *Courbet* saw action against the advancing German army in 1940, and were interned in Britain after the fall of France. *Paris* was offered to the Free Polish navy as a depot ship and finally scrapped in Brest in 1956. *Courbet* was a hulk, powered by an old railway locomotive lashed to her deck, when she was scuttled as a block ship off Ouistreham on the eastern edge of the Normandy landings where she was repeatedly attacked by German manned-torpedoes.

The French navy's operations in World War I were to convoy troops from North Africa to metropolitan France, then to counter the Italian and Austro-Hungarian fleets in the Mediterranean.

Courbet class

Class: *Courbet, Jean Bart, France, Paris.*
    Launched 1911–12
Dimensions: Length – 158.5m/520ft
    Beam – 27.89m/91ft 6in
    Draught – 8.99m/29ft 6in
Displacement: 22,545 tonnes/22,189 tons
Armament: Main – 12 x 305mm/12in guns
    Secondary – 22 x 135mm/5.4in guns and
    4 x 455mm/18in torpedoes
Machinery: 24 boilers, 4 shafts, power
    20,880kW/28,000shp
Speed: 20 knots
Complement: 1,085 men

When Italy joined the allies the French were released to support the allied landings at Gallipoli, while the Italians guarded the Austro-Hungarians. The Royal Navy was responsible for closing the Channel and North Sea to the Germans.

Bretagne class

These ships were developments of the Courbet class, but as French resources were increasingly directed towards her army, their completion was delayed and they saw little action during World War I.

The heavy guns were 340mm/13.5in, but instead of wing turrets they carried a centre-line midships turret which could fire on either beam. Unlike the Courbet class they were regularly modernized in the 1920s and 30s, during which they were converted to oil-burning, and the torpedo tubes and minelaying capability were suppressed. The after funnel was also raised. After trials in these ships with balloons and ramps in the 1930s, Lorraine's funnel was also moved aft and the midships turret removed so she could carry up to four aircraft.

All three ships operated with the British Mediterranean Fleet in early 1940. However, after the fall of France, the British demanded that the French navy should agree to measures of internment or disarmament to stop them falling into German hands, and when the French admiral at Mers-el-Kebir could not agree, Provence, Bretagne and other warships were shelled on July 3, 1940, by the British battleships Hood, Barham and Resolution. Bretagne blew up with large loss of life. Provence was sunk and then salvaged by the French, and taken to Toulon where she was scuttled in 1942 by patriotic Frenchmen. She was then raised by the Germans so that her guns could be installed in coastal batteries, and finally broken up in 1949.

In July 1940 Lorraine was in the British naval base of Alexandria, where she agreed to internment, and subsequently joined the Free French navy at Dakar in 1943. She took part in the Allied landings in southern France in 1944, bombarding French soil, and in 1945 in the reduction of a remaining German stronghold, near the mouth of the Gironde. She was scrapped in 1954.

The Vasilefs Konstantinos (also Re Constantino) was built in France for the Greek navy in 1914. She was very similar in design to the Provence class, and with the outbreak of war she was taken over by the French navy and given the name Savoie but never completed.

TOP: **French shipbuilding programmes were often leisurely and the Bretagne class took four years to complete, 1912–16.** ABOVE: **One of the class at a speed trial in 1914. The class saw little action in the war. Two ships suffered under the guns of the British, and a third ship was used to bombard southern France and ports along the French Atlantic coast.**

Bretagne class

Class: *Bretagne, Provence, Lorraine.*
   Launched 1913
Dimensions: Length – 164.9m/541ft
   Beam – 26.9m/88ft 3in
   Draught – 8.9m/29ft 2in
Displacement: 23,600 tonnes/23,230 tons
Armament: Main – 10 x 340mm/13.5in guns
   Secondary – 22 x 135mm/5.4in guns and
   4 x 455mm/18in torpedoes
Machinery: 24 boilers, 4 shafts,
   21,625kW/29,000shp
Speed: 20 knots
Complement: 1,124 men

Normandie class

In the midst of growing tension in Europe, France announced an ambitious programme in 1912 to achieve a strength of 28 battleships by 1922. It was envisaged that this would be reached by building battleships, and battlecruisers or fast battleships, in divisional numbers, of two and even three units per year. However, with the outbreak of World War I, France placed her priority for resources on her army and the Royal Navy was left to guard the northern flank of the allied armies on the Channel and North Sea coast. With this nearly all work on designing or building capital ships in France slowed to a stop.

Construction of five ships of the Normandie class began in 1913 and 1914. The French had also designed a quadruple 340mm/13.5in turret, which was planned for this class, and adoption of which would have enabled French designers to reduce the length and weight of the armoured citadel. This class would therefore have had three turrets, one each forward, midships and aft. Work continued as far as to allow the hulls to be launched, but thereafter they were robbed of their equipment, the boilers were taken for smaller warships and the guns for the army. Some of these guns were captured by the German army and turned against their builders. The hulls of *Normandie, Languedoc, Flandre* and *Gascogne* languished uncompleted for many years until the Washington Naval Treaty sealed their fate and they were deleted in 1922 from the French order of battle and scrapped. Work on *Vendée* recommenced in 1918 and after some experiments she was completed as the aircraft carrier *Béarn* in 1927.

Normandie class

Class: *Normandie, Vendée, Flandre, Gascogne, Languedoc.* Not launched

Dimensions: Length – 194.5m/638ft 2in
Beam – 29m/95ft 2in
Draught – 8.65m/28ft 5in

Displacement: 29,465 tonnes/29,000 tons

Armament: Main – 16 x 340mm/13.5in guns
Secondary – 24 x 135mm/5.4in guns and
6 x 455mm/18in torpedoes

Machinery: 21 or 28 boilers, 4 shafts,
23,862kW/32,000shp

Speed: 23 knots

Complement: 1,200 men

BELOW: **None of the Normandie class was completed, but one hull was taken to convert to France's first aircraft carrier, *Béarn*. She was too small and slow to be successful, although after conversion in World War II by the Americans she finished her career as a submarine tender, finally broken up in 1967.**

LEFT: **As a design, *Dante Alighieri* was clearly in the line of succession of Cuniberti's elegant proposals for the all-big-gun ship, and one which was copied by the Russian navy. This aerial photograph gives a very good idea of Cuniberti's concept: a relatively clear upper deck without large numbers of secondary or tertiary guns, and the main guns able to bear over wide angles of fire.** BELOW: **Firing a broadside from the midships two turrets.**

Dante Alighieri

The Italian warship designer Vittorio Cuniberti had already designed a number of ships for the Italian navy when he had published an article in *Jane's Fighting Ships* on what he thought would be the ideal battleship for the Royal Navy. This ship had 12 305mm/12in guns in single and double turrets and secondary armament was to consist of 75mm/3in guns. Cuniberti also placed emphasis on speed, sacrificing armour if need be, and proposed a ship which has a displacement of 17,273 tonnes/17,000 tons.

However, Admiral Fisher took up Cuniberti's all-big-gun idea in Britain, while Cuniberti and the Italian navy were still building distinctly pre-Dreadnought ships like the Vittorio Emanuele class. These were small battleships (13,209 tonnes/13,000 tons) with two single 305mm/12in guns in fore and aft mountings and a range of medium- and small-calibre guns. These ships were laid down in 1901–5 and although completed they took some six years each to build while the Italians absorbed intelligence about *Dreadnought*.

The Italian Government joined the Dreadnought race by authorizing the *Dante Alighieri* in 1907, although she was not laid down until 1909. The Cuniberti-designed ship had 12 305mm/12in guns, all on the centre line, one forward and one aft, and two amidships. A novel feature of the design was that the guns were for the first time in any navy placed in triple mountings. This arrangement enabled the boiler rooms to be widely separated and the engine room to be placed in the centre of the ship. *Dante Alighieri* also had two in-line rudders and four shafts. When completed she was capable of 24 knots and reckoned to be the fastest battleship in the world, although critics suggested that the armour was too light.

Dante Alighieri's only noteworthy action in World War I was the bombardment of Durazzo in the Adriatic during the army's struggle with the Austro-Hungarians. She was modified in 1923 and given a tripod foremast, taller

fore funnels and an aircraft ramp on C turret, but was scrapped in 1928.

The type was copied by the Russians in both their Gangut and Imperatrica Marija classes.

Dante Alighieri

Class: *Dante Alighieri*. Launched 1910.
Dimensions: Length – 158m/518ft 5in
 Beam – 26.6m/87ft 3in
 Draught – 8.8m/28ft 10in
Displacement: 19,835 tonnes/19,522 tons
Armament: Main – 12 x 305mm/12in guns
 Secondary – 20 x 120mm/4.7in,
 13 x 75mm/3in guns and
 3 x 455mm/18in torpedoes
Machinery: 23 boilers, 4 shafts,
 26,360kW/35,350shp
Speed: 24 knots
Complement: 950 men

Conte di Cavour class

These three ships were the epitome of Cuniberti's ideas. They carried a main armament of 305mm/12in guns and 18 120mm/4.7in guns in casements around the superstructure as defence against torpedo boats. The arrangement of the heavy guns was novel. The Italians adopted the principle of super-firing guns and placed a twin turret above a triple turret forward and aft, and also a triple turret amidships on the centre line, giving the unusual number of 13 main armament guns. This was only one gun less than the then most heavily armed ship in the world, the Brazilian 14-gun *Rio de Janeiro* (later the British *Agincourt*), but in two fewer turrets.

Critics again thought that these ships were too lightly armoured, and that, in the tradition of Italian warship building, too much had been sacrificed for speed. This was tacitly acknowledged in the inter-war years when heavier armour and the Pugliese system was fitted, but by then the output of the machinery had also been increased from 22,371kW/30,000hp to 67,113kW/90,000hp.

Conte di Cavour and *Giulio Cesare* were modified in the 1920s after the Washington Naval Treaty. The foremast was moved to a better position, before the fore funnel (a mistake the British had made in *Dreadnought* by placing the mast where it would be wreathed in funnel smoke) and both ships were fitted with catapults for aircraft. In one more demonstration of innovation in Italian design, the catapult was placed on the forecastle and the aircraft stored on the roof of the A turret.

Leonardo da Vinci sank as a consequence of an internal magazine explosion in 1916 at Taranto harbour, and although she was raised, was scrapped in 1921. This explosion was blamed on saboteurs, but it is more likely that it was one more in a series resulting from unstable ammunition. Neither *Conte di Cavour* nor *Giulio Cesare* saw any action in World War I, and they were so

TOP: **The silhouette was transformed when the Conte di Cavour class was modernized in the 1930s.**
ABOVE: ***Guilio Cesare*, followed by *Conte di Cavour*, off Naples for the Italian fleet review of 1938.** BELOW LEFT: **A rare picture of *Conte di Cavour* flying off her aircraft from the forecastle-mounted catapult.**

largely rebuilt, starting in 1933, and their appearance changed, that they also appear under separate entries in *Battleships of World War II*.

Conte di Cavour class

Class: *Conte di Cavour, Giulio Cesare, Leonardo da Vinci.* Launched 1911
Dimensions: Length – 168.9m/554ft 1in
Beam – 28m/91ft 10in
Draught – 9.3m/30ft 6in
Displacement: 23,360 tonnes/22,992 tons
Armament: Main – 13 x 305mm/12in guns
Secondary – 18 x 120mm/4.7in,
13 x 75mm/3in guns and
3 x 455mm/18in torpedoes
Machinery: 20 boilers, 4 shafts,
23,324kW/31,278shp
Speed: 22.2 knots
Complement: 1,197 men

Caio Duilio class

Similar in layout to the Conte di Cavour class with their two tall funnels and tripod mast mounted before each, these two ships had the trademark 13 heavy guns mounted in five turrets, and retained the medium guns in casements, but increased the calibre from 120mm/4.7in to 150mm/6in. This increased the displacement by 2,032 tonnes/2,000 tons without any serious adverse affects upon the speed of about 21 knots. Other Italian features included two in-line rudders. Neither ship saw action during World War I.

From 1926 onwards they carried an aircraft launched from a rail over the forecastle, and the familiar arrangement of rangefinders in Italian ships whereby they were mounted vertically one over the other revolving around the forward conning tower. *Caio Duilio* was damaged by an internal explosion in 1925, and with the *Andrea Doria* was rebuilt in the years 1937–40.

In 1914 Italy also ordered four larger battleships (29,465 tonnes/29,000 tons) *Francesco Morosini, Francesco Caracciolo, Cristoforo Colombo* and *Marcantonio Colonna* but work on these ships came to a halt during World War I. They were intended to be fast battleships, similar to but faster than the British Queen Elizabeth class, and a direct response to the Austro-Hungarian Ersatz Monarch class which were building in Triestino. The 380mm/15in guns intended for these ships were used in several monitors.

Under the Washington Naval Treaty Italy was allowed 71,120 tonnes/70,000 tons and plans were drawn up for three 23,370-tonne/23,000-ton 380mm/15in-gun battleships in 1928. This was partly in response to news of the French Dunkerque class, but eventually a larger design was chosen which became the Vittorio Veneto class.

TOP: *Caio Duilio* as she appeared in World War I, showing the classic lines of a Dreadnought battleship and her similarity to the contemporary British designs. ABOVE: Photographed in about 1912, the guns have been installed but the builders have not yet left or removed their mess.

Caio Duilio class

Class: *Caio Duilio, Andrea Doria.* Launched 1913
Dimensions: Length – 165.8m/544ft 1in
  Beam – 28m/91ft 10in
  Draught – 9.4m/30ft 10in
Displacement: 23,324 tonnes/22,956 tons
Armament: Main – 13 x 305mm/12in guns
  Secondary – 16 x 150mm/6in, 19 x 75mm/3in
  guns and 3 x 455mm/18in torpedoes
Machinery: 20 boilers, 4 shafts.
  22,371kW/30,000shp
Speed: 21 knots
Complement: 1,198 men

Gangut class

This class was a compromise. Whilst the Tsar wanted these ships, his Duma did not and the naval staff favoured a design by Cuniberti but a technical committee preferred a Blohm and Voss design. The German design was opposed on principle and John Brown and Co. from Britain was brought in to re-work the drawings. The resulting ship was a Baltic-Dreadnought, close to Cuniberti's original ideas. British (Yarrow) boilers instead of French (Belleville) boilers gave a speed of 24.5 knots on trials, at the expense of some armour and although the armour was thinner it was spread over the full hull. Ice-breaking bows were also fitted.

All four ships formed part of the Russian First Battleship Brigade based in the Baltic, where they conducted a series of minor operations until they came under Bolshevik control during the Russian Revolution, and were demobilized at Kronstadt in 1918.

Petropavlovsk engaged Royal Navy destroyers in May 1919, during British intervention in the Russian civil war, and on August 17 she was sunk by torpedoes from British coastal motor boats which raided Kronstadt harbour. She was raised and modernized between 1926–8 and participated in the 1937 fleet review at Spithead as *Marat*. In 1939 *Marat* bombarded Finnish positions, and in 1941 was hit by German long-range artillery and aerial bombs while alongside at Kronstadt, where she settled on the bottom. Partially repaired in January 1944, she was used as a fixed battery to fire on German army positions south of Kronstadt. She was renamed *Petropavlovsk* in 1943, and broken up in about 1953.

Poltava caught fire in 1922, sank and was plundered for spares for her sisters. Repairs were commenced on her under the name of *Frunze* in 1926–8 but she was hulked again in the 1930s. Her remains were sunk at Leningrad in 1941 and she was broken up in the 1950s.

Sevastopol operated with *Gangut* during World War I, and was modernized in 1928 as *Parizhkaya Kommuna*. While on passage to the Black Sea she was forced into Brest for repairs in 1929. She was modernized again in 1936–9 and during World War II bombarded the seaward flank of the advancing German army. She reverted to her old name in 1942, and was broken up in the late 1950s.

ABOVE: *Gangut* at anchor. A comparison with the aerial picture of *Dante Alighieri* shows how similar these ships are to the original Italian design. Considering their length and variety of service, these were successful and long-lived ships which withstood a great deal of damage.

Gangut was refitted in 1926–8 and 1931–4, and renamed *Oktyabrskaya Revolyutsiya*. In World War II she duelled with Finnish and then German positions, and on September 23, 1941, was hit by several bombs. Repaired at the Baltic Shipyard, she was ready to bombard the flank of the retreating German army in 1944. She was finally broken up in 1959.

Gangut class

Class: *Gangut, Petropavlovsk, Poltava, Sevastopol.* Launched 1911
Dimensions: Length – 180m/590ft 6in
  Beam – 26.6m/87ft 3in
  Draught – 8.4m/27ft 6in
Displacement: 23,735 tonnes/23,360 tons
Armament: Main – 12 x 305mm/12in guns
  Secondary – 16 x 120mm/4.7in guns and
  4 x 455mm/18in torpedoes
Machinery: 25 boilers, 4 shafts.
  31,319kW/42,000shp
Speed: 23 knots
Complement: 1,126 men

Imperatritsa Mariya class

Similar to the Ganguts but adapted for operations in the Black Sea, the Russian naval staff wanted bigger guns to counteract the battleships ordered in Britain for Turkey. However, to avoid delay in acquiring 355mm/14in guns, 305mm/12in main armament was accepted. John Brown and Co. advised in their construction as with the Ganguts. A heavier armoured belt was provided, but the problem of blast from the main guns affecting the secondary armament in its casemates was not resolved. There were minor differences between these ships when completed, and a bewildering series of name changes.

Imperatritsa Mariya bombarded the Turkish and Bulgarian coasts in 1915 and 1916 and on July 22, 1916, fought the ex-German Turkish-flagged light cruiser *Breslau*. On October 20, 1916, she suffered an internal explosion, whilst alongside in Sevastopol. Sabotage was suspected, but the most likely cause was a spontaneous explosion of unstable ammunition. The wreck was raised in 1918 and broken up in 1922.

Imperator Alexander III was not completed until after the Russian Revolution in February 1917, when she was renamed *Volya*. In April 1918, for a few months, she flew the flag of the independent state of Ukraine, but on October 1, 1918, she was seized by the Germans and renamed (perhaps

mistakenly) *Volya*. In 1919 she sailed briefly under the British flag, and during the war between the Red and White Russians she fought on the side of the Whites under the name of *General Alekseev*. She was steamed to Bizerta, where the French government offered to give her up to the newly installed Soviet rulers of Russia, but she was sold for scrapping in 1924 and finally broken up in 1936.

Imperatritsa Ekaterina Velikaya (ex *Ekaterina II*) also undertook bombardment operations, and she fought the ex-German battlecruiser *Goeben* on January 7–8, 1916, and the light cruiser *Breslau* on April 4–5, 1916. In April 29, 1917, she was renamed *Svobodnaya Rossiya* and under this name she again fought *Breslau* on June 24–5, 1917. Under the terms of the armistice she should have been handed

over to the Germans but escaped from Sevastopol to Novorossijsk where she was sunk by torpedoes from the destroyer *Kerch* on June 18, 1918.

Imperatritsa Mariya class

Class: *Imperatritsa Mariya, Imperator Alexander III, Ekaterina II.* Launched 1913–14

Dimensions: Length – 167.8m/550ft 6in
Beam – 27.3m/89ft 6in
Draught – 8.4m/27ft 6in

Displacement: 22,960 tonnes/22,600 tons

Armament: Main – 12 x 305mm/12in guns
Secondary – 20 x 130mm/5.1in guns and
4 x 455mm/18in torpedoes

Machinery: 20 boilers, 4 shafts.
19,761kW/26,500shp

Speed: 21 knots

Complement: 1,220 men

Imperator Alexander III renamed *Volya* and *Ekaterina II* renamed *Imperatritsa Ekaterina Velikaya*. *Ekaterina II* was slightly longer and larger than her sisters.

ABOVE: *Imperator Alexander III*, seen here from a distance, entered service after the February 1917 revolution in Russia, when she was renamed *Volya*. *Volya* later flew the flag of independent Ukraine and later still under White Russian authority she was known as *General Alexieff*. LEFT: *Volya* also spent some time under German and then British control as revolution raged around the Black Sea. The clean lines and minimum of superstructure, with the emphasis on keeping free the big guns' arcs of fire, show the influence of Italian design. Under German control she was briefly known as *Volga*.

LEFT: **Although the Bolsheviks renamed *Imperator Nikolai I* in 1917 and called her *Demokratiy*, she was never finished.**

Imperator Nikolai I

Intended as a fourth ship of the Imperatritsa Mariya class, *Imperator Nikolai I* was a larger ship all round, which enabled her designers to give her increased armour. She was built on the Black Sea and intended to counter the acquisition by Turkey of the *Rio de Janeiro* (which became the British *Agincourt*) from the Brazilian navy. Although 355mm/14in and even 400mm/16in guns were contemplated for this ship, the guns never became available. In any case, *Imperator Nikolai I* was not completed: she fell into German hands in 1918 and into the Allies' hands in 1919. Although the Germans started to break her, construction was later recommenced until the Allies decided to demolish her to prevent her being commissioned by the Reds.

Imperator Nikolai I	
Class: *Imperator Nikolai I.* Launched 1916	
Dimensions: Length – 188m/616ft 9in	
Beam – 28.9m/94ft 9in	
Draught – 9m/29ft 6in	
Displacement: 27,740 tonnes/27,300 tons	
Armament: Main – 12 x 305mm/12in guns	
Secondary – 20 x 130mm/5.1in guns and	
4 x 455mm/18in torpedoes	
Machinery: 20 boilers, 4 shafts.	
19,243kW/27,300shp	
Speed: 21 knots	
Complement: 1,252 men	

Borodino class

The Russian battleships and battlecruisers all had a similar silhouette, except that in the Borodino class the forward triple turret was carried one deck higher on an extended forecastle. The forward secondary guns in their casemates were still wet, and suffered from blast effects by continuing to be placed beneath the main turrets. As World War I developed the Russians had difficulty in sourcing equipment for the Borodino class, especially the turbines. None were completed. Consideration was given to converting the most advanced ship, *Izmail*, to an aircraft carrier but all were broken up.

Borodino class	
Class: *Borodino, Izmail, Kinburn, Navarin.*	
Launched 1915–16	
Dimensions: Length – 221.9m/728ft	
Beam – 30.5m/100ft	
Draught – 10.2m/33ft 6in	
Displacement: 33,020 tonnes/32,500 tons	
Armament: Main – 12 x 355mm/14in guns	
Secondary – 24 x 130mm/5.1in guns and	
6 x 535mm/21in torpedoes	
Machinery: 25 boilers, 4 shafts,	
50,708kW/68,000shp	
Speed: 26.5 knots	
Complement: 1,250 men	

LEFT: **Like other nations, the Russians named ships after famous victories on land. Borodino, sunk in 1905 was to have been replaced by one of four ships built at St Petersburg, but they were overwhelmed by the Russian revolution and never completed. Except in the Black Sea, the Russian navy never recovered from its defeat at the Battle of Tsushima.**

Radetzky class

These ships, the last of the Austro-Hungarian pre-Dreadnoughts, were designed by Siegfried Popper. Popper wanted to build an all-big-gun ship but could not fit the necessary gun layout into a ship of less than 16,257 tonnes/ 16,000 tons to which he was constrained by the size of the available docks.

Although small and seemingly over-armed for their displacement, the Radetzkys were well suited to warfare in the Adriatic, even if their active service was against shore targets rather than against other warships. Some speed was given up for increased armour, which was similar to British Dreadnoughts, while they were not much slower than their Italian equivalents. Popper emphasized underwater protection, and when underwater explosive experiments failed to inform him, he devised a satisfactory mathematical model for his design of an armoured double bottom.

Erzherzog Franz Ferdinand was named after the Austrian crown prince whose assassination at Sarajevo marked the start of World War I.

Radetzky was at the British Coronation Review in 1911 and all three ships of the class made training cruises in the eastern Mediterranean in 1912. In 1913 they formed part of an international squadron which demonstrated in the Ionian against the Balkan War.

In the spring of 1914 *Zrinyi* made a training cruise with the two new Dreadnoughts, *Viribus Unitis* and *Tegetthoff*, in the eastern Mediterranean and visited Malta.

In the opening moves of World War I, the Radetzkys covered the German Admiral Souchon's escape from the Adriatic, and bombarded Montenegro and Ancona and other coastal targets, but after the summer of 1915 they took little active part in the war.

Austro-Hungary wanted to give her fleet to the Yugoslavs in order to keep it out of Italian hands but *Erzherzog Franz Ferdinand* was interned at Venice. However Yugoslav officers steamed *Radetzky* and *Zrinyi* from Pola. On sighting a superior Italian force, the two battleships hoisted American flags and

ABOVE: **Not many pictures of the Austro-Hungarian fleet have survived: this is *Radetzky* photographed in 1911. Her only action was the bombardment of Ancona in Italy. She fell, briefly, into Yugoslav hands at the end of the war, but was allocated to the USA and scrapped in Italy.**

sailed south down the Adriatic coast to Split, where a flotilla of USN submarine chasers accepted their surrender. However, all three ships were eventually ceded to Italy and scrapped in 1920–6.

Radetzky class	
Class: *Erzherzog Franz Ferdinand, Radetzky, Zrinyi.* Launched 1908–10	
Dimensions: Length – 137.44m/450ft 11in	
Beam – 24.59m/80ft 8in	
Draught – 8.15m/26ft 9in	
Displacement: 14,740 tonnes/14,508 tons	
Armament: Main – 4 x 305mm/12in guns	
Secondary – 8 x 240mm/9.4in,	
20 x 100mm/4in guns and	
3 x 455mm/18in torpedoes	
Machinery: 12 Yarrow boilers, 2 shafts.	
14,765kW/19,800ihp	
Speed: 20.5 knots	
Complement: 876 men	

Tegetthoff class

The Tegetthoff class was the Austro-Hungarian response to news of the building of the Italian Dreadnought, *Dante Alighieri*. Although German experts had been consulted, the design was all-Austrian and the decision to fit triple turrets was influenced more by the desire to match the Italians. When financial authority for these ships was slow in forthcoming, the Austrian Commander-in-Chief, Admiral Montecuccoli, took out a personal loan for these ships, some months before parliament approved their construction.

The ships were compact, yet strongly armed and armoured. Their main weaknesses were the lack of reserve displacement and poor underwater protection, which led to the loss of two ships of the class.

In June 1918, Admiral Horthy planned a major raid on the Otranto barrage, in coordination with the Austro-Hungarian army. His battleships left Pola in two poorly protected groups: *Viribus Unitis* and *Prinz Eugen* on June 8, and *Szent Istvan* and *Tegetthoff* the next evening. *Szent Istvan*'s engines gave her trouble, reducing speed and making excessive smoke, and she was intercepted in the early hours of the morning by two Italian torpedo-boats on an unrelated mission

off the island of Premuda. *Szent Istvan* was hit with two torpedoes and the bulkhead between the boiler rooms collapsed. She quickly flooded and within three hours she had capsized. The sinking was filmed from *Tegetthoff*, making it one of the rare sequences of a battleship being sunk. The planned bombardment was aborted and the Austro-Hungarian navy returned to harbour for the last time.

On October 6, 1918, the Austrian emperor gave the Austro-Hungarian navy to the National Council of Slovenians, Croats and Serbs, and the fleet allegedly hoisted the Croatian flag. That night, while the end of the war was celebrated ashore and afloat, two Italian divers placed mines under the brightly lit *Viribus Unitis*, which blew up at dawn. Four days later Italian troops entered Pola and captured *Tegetthoff* and *Prinz Eugen*.

ABOVE: **One of the Tegetthoff class at speed. She was named after one of the few Austro-Hungarian naval leaders.** LEFT: *Szent Istvan* **was sunk by Italian torpedo-boats in 1918 and settled slowly, giving sufficient time for her loss to be filmed from her sister ship,** *Tegetthoff,* **and for some unique and poignant footage to be captured.**

Prinz Eugen was ceded to France and expended in underwater explosive tests as a bomb target and finally sunk by the guns of the French battleships *Jean Bart, Paris* and *France*. *Tegetthoff* was ceded to Italy and broken up in 1924–5.

In 1914–16 the Austro-Hungarian navy laid down four improved Tegetthoff ships, but these were never launched.

Tegetthoff class

Class: *Viribus Unitis, Tegetthoff, Prinz Eugen, Szent Istvan.* Launched 1911–14

Dimensions: Length – 151m/495ft 5in
Beam – 27.3m/89ft 8in
Draught – 8.9m/29ft

Displacement: 20,334 tonnes/20,013 tons

Armament: Main – 12 x 305mm/12in guns
Secondary – 12 x 150mm/6in,
18 x 65mm/2.6in guns and
4 x 535mm/21in torpedoes

Machinery: 12 boilers, 4 shafts
(*Szent Istvan* 2 shafts). 20,134kW/27,000shp

Speed: 20.5 knots

Complement: 1,087 men

LEFT: *Drottningen Victoria* is seen here during her sea trials in 1921. The photograph shows her as newly completed, but all three ships were modernized before World War II. ABOVE: Perhaps the most unusual flying accident occurred in 1939 when an aircraft crashed into the foremast of *Gustav V*. BELOW: An unusual photograph of a torpedo firing trial in 1893. Many battleships carried torpedoes in underwater tubes which were never photographed.

Sverige class

By the beginning of the 20th century Sweden possessed a large fleet although some of the hulls were elderly. Even the *John Ericsson*, which was almost 50 years old, having been upgraded three times, was still available. Between 1900 and 1905 the Swedish navy decided to build three classes of coast defence ships, Dristigheten, Oscar II and five ships of the Åran class.

However, Sweden's traditional enemy was Russia and larger ships were needed to increase the enemy's risk by forcing her to commit her own battleships in the event of an invasion. After considering a range of designs the so-called F-boat was decided upon in 1911, only for a change of government in 1912 to cancel the order on economic grounds. A remarkable battleship-club was started that rapidly raised more than enough money to build the first ship of a new class, and the government had little option but to thank the people and begin construction of *Sverige*.

The second and third ships of this class, *Drottningen Victoria* and *Gustaf V*, although ordered during World War I, were not completed until 1921 and 1922. The design of the later ships also changed slightly, they were larger and had two shafts instead of four and icebreaking stems instead of rams. After successive modernization all three ships differed from each other, all were given heavy tripod masts, but in *Gustaf V* the two funnels were combined into one, while *Sverige* was given an S-shaped fore funnel, and *Drottningen Victoria* retained her upright funnels. There were different arrangements of gun directors, and at each modernization the anti-aircraft weaponry was improved. Coal-fired boilers were also replaced by oil.

Swedish battleships successfully helped to safeguard their neutrality in two world wars, and the fate of other navies meant that for many years in the 20th century the Swedish navy was master of the Baltic, but by 1957 the Swedish battleships had been decommissioned. All that remains of Sweden's battleship ambitions are various guns which were set up in fixed defensive batteries.

Sverige class

Class: *Sverige, Drottningen Victoria, Gustaf V.*
Launched 1915–18
Dimensions: Length – 120.9m/396ft 8in
Beam – 18.6m/61ft
Draught– 6.2m/20ft 4in
Displacement: 7,240 tonnes/7,125 tons
(*Sverige* 6,935 tonnes/6,825 tons)
Armament: Main – 4 x 280mm/11in guns
Secondary – 8 x 150mm/6in, 6 x 75mm/3in guns
and 2 x 535mm/21in torpedoes
Machinery: 12 boilers, 2 shafts,
17,830kW/23,910shp
Speed: 22.5 knots
Complement: 427 men

De Zeven Provincien

While armed and armoured like a small battleship, *De Zeven Provincien* was in fact the last of the long line of Dutch coast defence ships. *De Zeven Provincien* saw little action in World War I, in which the Netherlands were neutral, and in 1912 was sent to the Dutch East Indies, the vast archipelago which later became Indonesia.

When a mutiny broke out onboard in 1933, *De Zeven Provincien* was bombed by a Dutch seaplane which hit her forecastle, killing 23 men. In 1935–6 she was used as a training ship, and in 1937 she was substantially modified and re-commissioned under the name *Soerabaia. De Zeven Provincien* was badly damaged in a Japanese air attack on February 18, 1942, and scuttled a few days later.

Meanwhile, a Dutch Royal Commission in 1912–13 recommended the building of a new fleet for the Royal Netherlands Navy to defend the Netherlands, protect her colonies and police the East Indies. The fleet would have included nine battleships of about 20,320 tonnes/20,000 tons and capable of 21 knots, armed with 340mm/13.5in guns. The number of ships was determined by the perceived need to maintain a squadron in the Far East, a squadron in home waters, and a reserve. It was a long-term, rolling programme which envisaged the earlier ships being replaced by more modern ships over a 30-year period.

The Dutch got as far as asking German and British firms for proposals when World War I broke out and these plans were abandoned. The leading design was by Germaniawerft and provided for a ship of 21,000 tonnes/20,668 tons, 21 knots, and armed with eight 340mm/13.5in, 16 150mm/6in and 12 75mm/3in guns.

De Zeven Provincien class

Class: *De Zeven Provincien.* Launched 1909
Dimensions: Length – 101.5m/333ft
  Beam – 17.1m/56ft
  Draught – 6.2m/20ft 3in
Displacement: 6,635 tonnes/6,530 tons
Armament: Main – 2 x 280mm/11in and
  4 x 150mm/6in guns
  Secondary – 10 x 75mm/3in guns
Machinery: 8 boilers, 2 shafts,
  5,966kW/8,000ihp
Speed: 16 knots
Complement: 452 men

ABOVE: **The Dutch contemplated building a proper battleship, but only managed a coast defence ship, which they armed with 280mm/11in guns. She survived from 1910 to 1942.** LEFT: **One of the smallest post-Dreadnoughts to appear in these pages,** *De Zeven Provincien* **saw much of her service in the Dutch East Indies, where she was scuttled to prevent her falling into Japanese hands.** *De Zeven Provincien* **lies in the line of development between the pocket battleship and the monitor.**

España class

These three small battleships were built in Spain to British plans and largely under the supervision of British architects. The intention of their ingenious design was to incorporate the Dreadnought principles of an all-big-gun warship into the size of a pre-Dreadnought battleship. This was typical of a long tradition that British designers could be so adventurous with designs for foreign navies while at home the Admiralty was much more cautious about innovation. At less than 16,257 tonnes/16,000 tons they were the smallest and slowest Dreadnoughts and the variant was not copied elsewhere.

Their eight 305mm/12in guns were mounted in one turret forward and aft and two midships turrets mounted *en echelon*. The secondary armament was mounted in casemates. Distinctive recognition features were the boats mounted on the roofs of the midships turrets, the single upright funnel almost in the centre of the ship, and two tall tripod masts.

España ran aground off Morocco in 1923 and her large-calibre guns were salvaged but the wreck was broken up in the heavy surf which pounds that coast almost continually throughout the year.

Jaime I was not completed before the outbreak of World War I, when Britain was unable to supply further material. In 1923–5 she took part in what was known as the Riff revolt and was hit from a shore battery. In the Spanish Civil War she fought on the side of the Republicans, and bombarded Ceuta and Algeciras, but she was bombed in Malaga in 1936 and further damaged by an internal explosion in 1937. She was finally scrapped in 1939.

Alfonso XIII, which took the name *España* in 1931, declared for the Nationalists in the Spanish Civil War and bombarded Bilbao in April 1937, but soon afterwards hit a mine and was sunk – though at the time the Nazis claimed one of their aircraft had been involved.

Three more ships of a class named *Reina Eugenia* were supposed to be laid down during World War I, but plans were abandoned in favour of more affordable cruisers and destroyers. During World War II Franco approved a plan to build four modern battleships but financial weakness prevented this being taken up.

TOP: **A handsome picture of one of the España class (probably the renamed *Alfonso XIII* which was renamed *España* after the name ship had been wrecked) which shows a passing resemblance to Italian and Russian designs and faithfulness to Cuniberti's concepts.** ABOVE: ***España* declared for the nationalist government and was sunk by a mine off Santander. At the time the Germans thought that Basque government aircraft were responsible for the loss.**

España class

Class: *España, Jaime I, Alfonso XIII.*
   Launched 1912–14
Dimensions: Length – 132.58m/435ft
   Beam – 24m/78ft 9in
   Draught – 7.77m/25ft 6in
Displacement: 15,700 tonnes/15,453 tons
Armament: Main – 8 x 305mm/12in guns
   Secondary – 20 x 100mm/4in guns
Machinery: 12 boilers, 4 shafts.
   11,558kW/15,500shp
Speed: 19.5 knots
Complement: 854 men

Kilkis and *Lemnos*

*K*ilkis and *Lemnos* were both 13,209-tonne/13,000-ton battleships, originally built as two of the Mississippi class pre-Dreadnoughts completed in 1908 for the USN. Their place might properly be regarded as belonging to an earlier period, but they had careers that spanned both World Wars of the 20th century. The Greeks and Turks fought at sea in the Balkan Wars 1912–13, which saw the first use of aviation in modern warfare and the first use of submarine torpedo attack.

The Hellenic navy consisted of ships bought in from several navies, and two battleships were ordered, one from Germany and the other from France, but neither ship was finished. The American 355mm/14in guns intended for a German-built ship named *Salamis* were purchased for the British Abercrombie class monitors, and the unfinished *Salamis* was not scrapped until 1932. An unnamed French-built battleship of

23,369 tonnes/23,000 tons was to have been similar to the Provence class.

However, Greece did purchase two pre-Dreadnoughts from the USA in 1914, while Turkey hoped to acquire modern battleships from Britain. *Kilkis*, the name ship of the class, was taken over at Newport News, Virginia, in July and served in the Royal Hellenic Navy until 1932 when she became a training ship. *Lemnos* was in the Mediterranean on a training cruise with USN midshipmen when she was handed over.

The *Lemnos* was originally the *Idaho* and she was amongst the Greek naval ships temporarily seized by France in 1916 during a constitutional crisis in Greece. *Lemnos* was active in Turkish waters during the chaotic period following the end of World War I, but went out of active service during the 1930s and was retained as a hulk. *Kilkis* and her sister ship *Lemnos* became two of the longest-surviving

pre-Dreadnoughts until they were both sunk at Salamis by German dive-bombers on April 23, 1941, during the German invasion of Greece. The wrecks were salvaged for scrap in the 1950s.

LEFT: *Kilkis* and *Lemnos* retained the lattice masts which the USN had fitted before World War I. Apart from two Argentinian battleships built to order in the USA, they were the only USN battleships to pass out of American service and to fly a foreign flag.
ABOVE: Both ships were sunk by German aircraft while at anchor at Salamis in 1941. The picture was taken from a German bomber as it dived on *Kilkis* at anchor. The ships had not been modernized and were no match for modern air power.

Kilkis class

Class: *Kilkis* (ex *Idaho*), *Lemnos* (ex *Mississippi*). Launched 1905
Dimensions: Length – 116.4m/382ft
 Beam – 23.5m/77ft
 Draught – 7.5m/24ft 8in
Displacement: 13,210 tonnes/13,000 tons
Armament: Main – 4 x 305mm/12in,
 8 x 205mm/8in and 8 x 180mm/7in guns
 Secondary – 12 x 75mm/3in guns and
 2 x 535mm/21in torpedoes
Machinery: 8 boilers, 2 shafts,
 7,457kW//10,000ihp
Speed: 17 knots
Complement: 744 men

Yavuz Sultan Selim

The Turks had two old German pre-Dreadnought battleships, *Kurfürst Friedrich Wilhelm* and *Weissenburg*, which had been modernized and renamed as *Heireddin Barbarossa* and *Turgut Reis* and saw active service in World War I. *Heireddin Barbarossa* was sunk by the British submarine *E-11* in the Sea of Marmara on August 8, 1915. *Turgut Reis* survived as a hulk until she was broken up in 1956–7.

The Turks made several attempts to improve their battleship strength by purchasing ships in Britain. However, *Resadiye* was confiscated by the Royal Navy and commissioned as *Erin*, and two other ships of this class, *Mahmud Resad V* and *Fatik* were cancelled. *Sultan Osman I* (ex *Rio de Janeiro*) was also taken over as *Agincourt*.

Consequently, when the German battlecruiser *Goeben* and the cruiser *Breslau* escaped from the British Mediterranean Fleet, arriving off Istanbul on August 10, 1914, it was natural that the Turks were interested in acquiring these ships. *Goeben* transferred to the Turkish flag six days later, while retaining most of her German crew and thereafter led perhaps the busiest and longest life of any ship of the period.

Goeben was twice bested by the Russian Black Sea pre-Dreadnought squadron. On November 18, 1914, and again in May 1915, she exchanged fire with *Evstafi*, which hit *Goeben*, whereupon the German-Turkish ship again had to use her speed to avoid being outgunned by the Russian squadron.

On January 20, 1918, this time in the Dardanelles, *Goeben* sank the British monitors *Lord Raglan* and *M-28* but as the German-Turkish ships shaped a course for Lemnos island, *Breslau* hit a mine, and while *Goeben* attempted a tow *Goeben* hit three mines herself, while *Breslau* hit several more and sank rapidly. *Goeben* then ran aground on Nagara Point, where she was attacked by British seaplanes from *Ark Royal,* but the bombs used were too small to be effective. The British submarine *E-14* was diverted from her patrol in the Otranto Straits but by the time she arrived, *Goeben* had been towed off by *Turgut Reiss*.

Yavuz survived under the Turkish flag until 1973–6 when she was broken up shortly before her diamond jubilee – one of the longest surviving ships of her era.

LEFT: **The German battlecruiser *Goeben* was sold to the Turks in 1914 and is here seen under a prominent Turkish flag, although the German crew remained onboard to man her. She was not finally handed over to the Turkish authorities until November 1918.**
BELOW: **Under her new owners – whatever the nationality of the crew – *Yavuz Sultan Selim* took part in many actions in the Black Sea. In 1918, during a brief sortie from the Black Sea, she sank the British monitor *Raglan*.**

Yavuz Sultan Selim

Class: *Yavuz* (as *Goeben*). Launched 1910
Dimensions: Length – 186.5m/611ft 11in
    Beam – 29.5m/96ft 10in
    Draught – 9m/29ft 5in
Displacement: 22,979 tonnes/22,616 tons
Armament: Main – 10 x 280mm/11in guns
    Secondary – 12 x 150mm/6in,
    12 x 88mm/3.46in guns and
    4 x 510mm/20in torpedoes
Machinery: 24 boilers, 4 shafts,
    38,776kW/52,000shp
Speed: 25.5 knots
Complement: 1,053 men

Rivadavia class

In the 1870s the Argentine navy consisted of a few cruisers, and although *La Plata* (1874), *Los Andes* (1874), *Libertad* (1890), and *Independencia* (1891) were classed as coast defence battleships they were small and poorly armed. Only *Patagonia* (1885), a protected cruiser built in Italy, had a single gun of 255mm/10in size and she was reconstructed in 1909 as a survey ship. However, when Argentina's quarrel with Chile over boundaries in Patagonia and territorial limits in the Beagle Channel was settled (for the time being) by British arbitration in 1902, the British thoughtfully wrote into the treaty clauses concerning the limitation of naval arms. The Royal Navy bought two pre-Dreadnought battleships from Chile which were under construction in Britain and Argentina sold two cruisers to Japan which were building in Italy.

In 1904 the Brazilian Government decided upon a programme of naval expansion, and Argentina asked foreign companies to tender plans for new battleships. Fore River won the competition and the ships became the only Dreadnoughts built in the United States for a foreign navy. Although the Argentine decision was based on technical and financial grounds, there was another, unintended consequence of choosing American yards. Unlike orders placed by foreign nations in European yards where the ships being built were taken over by the warring powers, American neutrality during the early years of World War I allowed a timely delivery of both Dreadnoughts. As a result Argentina got her warships, whereas Brazil and Chile did not.

They were a combination of ideas from capital ship design, with battleship and battlecruiser features, good protection, significant armament and relatively high speed. The superimposed turret arrangement was American, and the wing turrets showed British design influence. The secondary 150mm/6in battery was attributed to German influence as were the triple shafts, but engine-room and boiler-room layout was similar to the Italian Dante Alighieri class. The forward cage mast was entirely American.

ABOVE: *Rivadavia* and *Moreno* were possibly the only major warships to be built in the USA for export. Their design incorporated features from American, British, German and Italian naval architecture. This picture shows the profile after modernization.

Both ships underwent modernization in the 1920s. In 1937 *Moreno* attended the Coronation Review at Spithead while *Rivadavia* tactfully visited Brest, and later both ships visited Wilhelmshaven. Neither ship fired her guns in anger during World War II, and in 1956 they were stricken from the navy list.

Rivadavia class

Class: *Rivadavia, Moreno.* Launched 1911
Dimensions: Length – 181.3m/594ft 9in
  Beam – 30m/98ft 4in
  Draught – 8.4m/27ft 8in
Displacement: 28,388 tonnes/27,940 tons
Armament: Main – 12 x 305mm/12in guns
  Secondary – 12 x 150mm/6in, 16 x 100mm/4in
  guns and 2 x 535mm/21in torpedoes
Machinery: 18 boilers, 3 shafts,
  29,455kW/39,500shp
Speed: 22.5 knots
Complement: 1,130 men

Minas Gerais class

Minas Gerais and Sao Paulo were the most powerful warships in the world when completed. They were built amid rumours that they were destined for another power, or for the Royal Navy, and had two super-firing turrets fore and aft and two wing turrets. The Brazilian Government ordered them even before the first Dreadnought was commissioned. The only outdated thing about these ships was that they were powered by reciprocating engines and not turbines. As a direct consequence the USA started to court Brazil as a pan-American ally, but a downturn in the economy and a mutiny halted the Brazilian Dreadnought programme. Therefore, when Brazil declared war on the Central Powers in 1917 and promised to send her battleships to join the Grand Fleet at Scapa Flow, both ships were in need of refit. Sao Paulo was sent to New York in June 1918 to be modernized, and though her refit outlasted the war, Minas Gerais was also sent north and completed her refit in 1923.

Minas Gerais was modernized in 1934–7, but Sao Paulo was judged to be in too poor a condition to justify the cost. Neither ship saw action in World War II. Sao Paulo, en route to Britain for breaking, broke her tow in the North Atlantic in 1951 and was never seen again. Minas Gerais was towed to Italy to be broken up in 1954.

In 1910 Brazil ordered a yet more powerful warship, which would have been the largest in the world. However a mutiny in the navy had undermined public support for buying Dreadnoughts, and eventually Rio de Janeiro was sold to Turkey as Sultan Osman I, and was about to be steamed away from Britain when the Royal Navy confiscated her under the name of Agincourt. In 1921 Great Britain offered to sell Agincourt back to Brazil but after consideration the idea was rejected.

The Brazilians contemplated a fourth Dreadnought, to be known as Riachuelo, and four designs were considered for a battleship of 32,005 tonnes/31,500 tons

TOP: *Sao Paulo* as built and photographed at Rio de Janeiro in 1918. ABOVE: *Minas Gerais*, date unknown, but showing features of World War I, the range clock, and World War II, what appear to be radar domes. BELOW LEFT: *Minas Gerais* in 1909. The structure apparently extending to port and starboard are in fact spans of the bridge over the River Tyne in England, where this was photographed.

to 36,580 tonnes/36,000 tons with main batteries of 355mm/14in, 380mm/15in or 405mm/16in guns. Construction was never started and the idea was dropped on the outbreak of World War I.

Minas Gerais class

Class: *Minas Gerais, Sao Paulo.* Launched 1908–9
Dimensions: Length – 165.5m/543ft
   Beam – 25.3m/83ft
   Draught – 7.6m/25ft
Displacement: 20,378 tonnes/19,281 tons
Armament: Main – 12 x 305mm/12in guns
   Secondary – 22 x 120mm/4.7in and
   8 x 3pdr guns
Machinery: 18 boilers, 2 shafts,
   17,524kW/23,500shp
Speed: 21 knots
Complement: 900 men

TOP: *Almirante Latorre* in 1913. Soon after this photograph she was purchased by the Royal Navy and renamed *Canada*. ABOVE: *Almirante Cochrane* at the time of her launch. In 1917 the uncompleted hull was purchased and finished by the British as the aircraft carrier *Eagle*.

Almirante Latorre class

As part of the South American naval arms race, Chile ordered two Dreadnoughts to counter the ships that the Argentine had built in face of the perceived threat from Brazil. The first ship was named *Valparaíso*, then *Libertad*, and thirdly *Almirante Latorre*. Work on *Almirante Latorre* started in 1911, but ironically work could not start on *Almirante Cochrane* until the Brazilian *Rio de Janeiro* had left the slip. The design was similar to the British Iron Duke class but with 355mm/14in guns in lieu of 340mm/13.5in, however neither ship was delivered to the Chileans.

At the outbreak of World War I the Royal Navy purchased *Almirante Latorre* from its ally and renamed her *Canada*, and for a while considered purchasing *Almirante Cochrane* to be renamed *India*. Being less advanced, work was halted on *Almirante Cochrane* until 1917, when she was taken in hand to be finished as

the aircraft carrier *Eagle*. *Almirante Latorre* (*Canada*) was modified at the end of the war and flying-off ramps were fitted over B and X turrets.

Chile finally took over *Canada* and gave her back her original name. The Chilean navy also wanted their second Dreadnought and asked for *Eagle* to be reconverted, but they were offered instead the battlecruiser *Inflexible*. This was refused and the Chileans settled for just one capital ship and several minor war vessels.

Almirante Latorre was modernized in Devonport in 1929–31 and converted to oil-fired boilers. Anti-torpedo bulges were fitted which raised her beam to 31.4m/103ft, and she was given new gunnery control systems. An Italian-designed catapult was fitted on the quarterdeck. She remained in service until 1958 when she was towed to Japan to be broken up.

Almirante Latorre class

Class: *Almirante Latorre* (as *Canada*), *Almirante Cochrane*. Launched 1913
Dimensions: Length – 201.47m/661ft
Beam – 28.04m/92ft
Draught – 8.84m/29ft
Displacement: 29,060 tonnes/28,600 tons
Armament: Main – 10 x 355mm/14in guns
Secondary – 16 x 150mm/6in guns and
4 x 535mm/21in torpedoes
Machinery: 21 boilers, 4 shafts,
27,591kW/37,000shp
Speed: 23 knots
Complement: 1,167 men

Glossary

aft At or towards the rear or stern.

battle cruiser Ship armed with battleship-sized guns, but in which armour has been dispensed with for speed and manoeuvrability.

beam The widest part of a ship.

bilge The lowest part of the hull of a ship, where the side turns into the bottom.

bilge keel Fins or narrow wings at the turn of the bilge, designed to improve stability.

blister *See* bulge.

bow (or bows) The forward end of a ship.

breastwork raised armoured bulkhead to protect a gun and its moving parts.

bulge (or blister) A longitudinal space, subdivided and filled with fuel, water or air, to protect against the effects of a torpedo hit.

bulkhead The internal vertical structures within a ship.

calibre The internal diameter or bore of a gun, or the ratio of the barrel length to the bore.

capital ship A generic name given to the largest and most powerful ships in a navy.

cofferdam Watertight bulkhead separating and protecting magazines and engine rooms.

Copenhagen Reference to the British attack on the Danish capital and fleet in 1807.

dressed overall A ship dressed *en fête*, flying lines of flags. between her masts, when not underway.

dwarf bulkhead Low bulkhead intended to stop the free flood of water.

flotilla A squadron in the Royal Navy before NATO standardization.

flying deck A deck suspended between two parts of the superstructure so that the deck below can be kept clear for mounting guns.

forecastle Forward part of a ship.

freeboard Height of the deck above the waterline.

gunwales Upper edge of the side of a vessel.

heel Lean or tilt of a ship.

ihp Indicated horsepower: the calculated output of a ship's machinery.

laid down Reference to when a new ship was first placed on the construction slip.

line ahead When ships form up in a line.

line-of-battle ship A ship large enough to be in the line.

metacentre Roll and return to upright slowly.

monitor Low freeboard coast defence vessel.

ordnance Armament and ammunition of a ship.

pole mast A stick-like mast to carry aerials or flags.

port Left side.

quarter Between the beam and the stern.

screw Propellor.

shp Shaft horse power: the actual measured output of a ship's machinery.

starboard Right side.

stern Rear of a ship.

theatre The area in which a ship or fleet operates or a naval campaign takes place.

tripod mast A mast having extra legs to carry the weight of direction-finding and gunnery control positions.

tumblehome Inward curve of a ship's side above the waterline.

turret Revolving armoured gun house.

USN United States Navy.

van The front of a formation of ships.

Key to flags

For the specification boxes, the national flag that was current at the time of the ship's use is shown.

 Argentina

 Austro-Hungary

 Brazil

 Chile

 France

 Germany

 Greece

 Italy

 Japan

 Netherlands

 Spain

 Sweden

 Turkey

 United Kingdom

 USA

 USSR

Acknowledgements

The publisher would like to thank the following individuals and picture libraries for the use of their pictures in the book. Every effort has been made to acknowledge the pictures properly, however we apologize if there are any unintentional omissions, which will be corrected in future editions. l=left, r=right, t=top, b=bottom, m=middle, lm= lower middle

Alinari Archives-Florence: Malandrini Ferruccio); 78t (De Pinto Donazione); 78m; 79t (De Pinto Donazione); 79b (De Pinto Donazione); 80t (De Pinto Donazione); 80m (De Pinto Donazione).

Australian War Memorial: 25mr (H12319); 38t (300238); 38b (ART09749).

Cody Images: 1; 2–3; 5; 6t; 6m; 7tl; 7tr; 7mr; 8–9; 15b; 16t; 16bl; 17tr; 17mr; 17br; 18; 19t; 19ml; 19mr; 20b; 21t; 21mr; 21br; 22t; 23tl; 23tr; 24t; 25bl; 27ml; 32t; 32m; 32b; 33b; 34; 36tl; 36tr; 36mr; 41mr; 44b; 45ml; 46mr; 47tl; 47tr; 48mr; 49br; 51t; 52t; 53tl; 53tr; 53mr; 56tl; 57t; 57b; 58b; 59t; 62b; 63tl; 63m; 65t; 65m; 66t; 66m; 66mr; 67mr; 67b; 68tl; 68tr; 68m; 69t; 69m; 70tl; 70tr; 70mr; 70b; 71mr; 71b; 72t; 72mr; 73t; 73m; 74–5t; 74br; 75m; 79mr; 81t; 83b; 88t; 88mr; 89mr; 89bl; 90m; 90b; 91t; 92t; 92mr; 94t; 94b; 95; 96b.

Mary Evans Picture Library: 17ml; 25ml; 62t.

Syd Goodman: 39ml; 39mr; 39bl; 46t; 48t; 49m; 54b; 55t; 76t.

Imperial War Museum Photograph Archive: 10 (Q68264); 11m (MH24467); 13t (Q13942); 13m (Q13941A); 14bl (Q55499); 14br (Q22156); 15tr (Q22155); 20tr (Q38938); 23tr (Q22687); 27t (Q20613); 61t (Q22411); 64b (MH6158); 82m (Q20283); 82b (Q20287); 84 (Q22227).

Institute for Maritime History: 86tl; 86tr; 86mr; 87ml; 87b.

Library of Congress: 11tr.

Maritime Prints and Originals: 22b (Courtesy of Michael French Esq.); 24m (Courtesy of Captain R. A. de S. Cosby LVO RN); 31t (Courtesy of Paul Winter Esq.); 33mr (Courtesy of Captain R. A. de S. Cosby LVO RN); 35t (Courtesy of Commander W. A. E. Hall RN); 45t (Courtesy of Simon Keeble Esq.).

North Sands Picture Library: 28; 41lm; 43m; 92bl; 93t; 93m.

Novosti: 83t.

Curt Ohlsson: 86tl; 86tr; 86mr.

Royal Naval Museum: 35m; 37t; 40t; 40mr; 41b; 42lm; 42b; 43t; 45mr; 50t; 51mr.

Erwin Sieche: 85t; 85b.

Topfoto: 61ml.

US Naval Historical Center: 26t; 26mr; 27t; 55ml; 55mr; 56tr; 56mr; 58t; 59tr; 59ml; 59mr; 60tl; 60ml; 64t; 65mr

Walker Archive: 12; 76mr.

Index